A CELL CALL
from
PAUL

MODERN MESSAGES FROM
FIRST-CENTURY PRISON LETTERS

David Waddell

WestBow Press
A DIVISION OF THOMAS NELSON
& ZONDERVAN

Melissa, I feel so blessed by God to have such an incredible friend like you in my life. You are unique, in a good way, and have the ability to brighten any day. Enjoy my new published craziness!

David Waddell
4/12/22

Copyright © 2022 David Waddell.

All rights reserved. No part of this book may be used or reproduced by any means, graphic, electronic, or mechanical, including photocopying, recording, taping or by any information storage retrieval system without the written permission of the author except in the case of brief quotations embodied in critical articles and reviews.

This book is a work of non-fiction. Unless otherwise noted, the author and the publisher make no explicit guarantees as to the accuracy of the information contained in this book and in some cases, names of people and places have been altered to protect their privacy.

WestBow Press books may be ordered through booksellers or by contacting:

WestBow Press
A Division of Thomas Nelson & Zondervan
1663 Liberty Drive
Bloomington, IN 47403
www.westbowpress.com
844-714-3454

Because of the dynamic nature of the Internet, any web addresses or links contained in this book may have changed since publication and may no longer be valid. The views expressed in this work are solely those of the author and do not necessarily reflect the views of the publisher, and the publisher hereby disclaims any responsibility for them.

Any people depicted in stock imagery provided by Getty Images are models, and such images are being used for illustrative purposes only.
Certain stock imagery © Getty Images.

Scripture quotations marked (NLT) are taken from the Holy Bible, New Living Translation, copyright ©1996, 2004, 2015 by Tyndale House Foundation. Used by permission of Tyndale House Publishers, a Division of Tyndale House Ministries, Carol Stream, Illinois 60188. All rights reserved.

Scripture quotations taken from The Holy Bible, New International Version® NIV® Copyright © 1973 1978 1984 2011 by Biblica, Inc.
TM. Used by permission. All rights reserved worldwide.

ISBN: 978-1-6642-5742-9 (sc)
ISBN: 978-1-6642-5744-3 (hc)
ISBN: 978-1-6642-5743-6 (e)

Library of Congress Control Number: 2022902701

Print information available on the last page.

WestBow Press rev. date: 03/01/2022

Contents

Introduction   vii

EPHESIANS   1

Chapter 1:3–14	First Draft Pick Chosen	2
Chapter 1:15–23	Prayers Are Paul's Specific Ocean	6
Chapter 2:1–10	You're Not That Bad	11
Chapter 2:11–22	The More We Get Together	15
Chapter 3:1–13	You Guys, Youins, and All Y'all	19
Chapter 3:14–21	Often Is Heard an Encouraging Word	24
Chapter 4:1–16	One for All and All for One	28
Chapter 4:17–32	Shedding Old Skin	33
Chapter 5:1–20	Dead Skunk Memories	38
Chapter 5:21–6:4	Wait! What's in It for Me?	42
Chapter 6:5–9	Employee Handbook	47
Chapter 6:10–24	Getting Ready to Get Ready	51

PHILIPPIANS   57

Chapter 1:3–11	A Silent Minute for Those Closest to Me	58
Chapter 1:12–19	A Different Kind of Prison	63
Chapter 2:1–18	Freedom in Accountability	67
Chapter 2:19–30	There's No I in Team	71
Chapter 3:1–11	What Is Really Important Here	76

Chapter 3:12–21	Archery, with No Target, Gives One the Shaft	80
Chapter 4:2–9	Don't Worry. Be Happy.	84
Chapter 4:10–20	The State in Which I Live	88

COLOSSIANS 93

Chapter 1:1–14	Good News or Good News	94
Chapter 1:15–23	Mirror Image	98
Chapter 1:24–29	My Pain—Your Gain	102
Chapter 2:1–5	A New Hope	106
Chapter 2:6–23	What Is the Rule about Rules?	110
Chapter 3:1–17	Clothing Makes the Man!	114
Chapter 3:18–4:1	Who's the Boss?	118
Chapter 4:2–6	If You Can't Say Anything Nice	122
Chapter 4:7–18	Pass the Baton to the Team	126

PHILEMON 131

Chapter 1	The Lender Becomes the Prisoner	132

Conclusion 137

Introduction

Contentment in Confinement

I'm a social person. I like to hang out with friends, meet new people, and make new friends. I had an excellent opportunity to be outgoing and social until the COVID-19 coronavirus hit our world. At that point, being alone at home became my new reality.

Like many, I found the time to get a few things done that had been waiting until I could find the time to complete them. So, I continued my work on this book, keeping my writing theme of taking the Bible personally. I believe the best-selling book in all of history reflects my life through the characters and the writing found inside the book. The inspiration for this selection came from a sermon series out of Ephesians in my home church. I shared the book's premise with my friend Tim Turner, and he wondered if my inspiration might have been to write about Paul's lockup during my lockdown. I told him it wasn't but that I would steal his idea on the subject and use it anyway.

While Paul was under house arrest in Rome, he wrote letters to the people and churches where he had visited and ministered. Some theologians refer to these as the Prison Letters, which I, and my passion for wordplay, renamed "A Cell Call from Paul." Paul, who had the blessing of prison doors opening up from an earthquake (Acts 16:25–26), also learned the blessings of being in a prison where he did not receive a miraculous delivery. My love of wordplay is so strong that a friend of mine correctly accused me of coming up with the title first and then writing the book.

At the time of Paul's cell call, Ephesus was a commercial and religious center of Asia Minor. Paul visited during his second missionary journey. It was a short visit, as he had come from Corinth and was going to Jerusalem and Antioch (Acts 18:18–21).

The church in Philippi sent Epaphroditus to Rome with some financial assistance for Paul. It was the return trip that Epaphroditus carried Paul's letter back to the church. Paul had visited this church on his second journey and the third journey as well.

The church at Colossae, planted by a man named Epaphras, was located east of Ephesus. Ironically, Paul had never visited this church. He had heard of the false teaching and heresy that were taking place when Epaphroditus came to visit. The heresy involved a combination of Greek speculation, Oriental mysticism, and Jewish legalism.

Philemon is not the name of a church or a town like the other three letters. Philemon is a man who lived in Colossae. He owned a slave named Onesimus, who had escaped and run away to Rome. He sought refuge with Paul, who then wrote the letter to his owner about forgiving Onesimus rather than punishing him or killing him.[1]

Similar to my other books, each chapter or story stands on its own. You don't need to read them in order. Instead, you may pick and choose the chapter or chapters that serve you best. Paul used similar themes in his cell call, and I have used some of the same stories or illustrations with different twists in this book. Please know, in some of the footnotes, I note a change in words to a more appropriate one for printing. The change was not due to the original quote using a swear word, but instead, a word found inappropriate by the publisher.

Paul's cell call is still an appropriate message for us today. While Paul was in a physical lockdown, his spirit soared freely. We all spend time in figurative prisons. I followed the same organization of thought as chapters and subjects in Paul's four letters while in prison. I believe we'll see our contentment in confinement grow as Paul's guidance and wisdom leads us back to the basics of our faith.

---

[1] https://www.christianity.com/wiki/bible/what-are-the-prison-epistles.html.

PAUL'S LETTER TO THE
EPHESIANS

Having lived several years in Memphis, Tennessee, I saw the value of having the intersection of two interstate highways, a major international airport, and access to a major waterway in the Mississippi River. Due to all the entrances and exits, several companies found it advantageous to place their headquarters or shipping centers in the city. Being the hometown to FedEx certainly didn't hurt the city's growth.

Ephesus was in many ways like modern-day Memphis. It sat on the shore of modern-day Turkey and had three major highways coming into the city. It was known as a vital trading center in the area. During the day of Roman reign, it was second only to the city of Rome for being a center of culture and commerce.[2]

The city was also known as a religious center of western Asia. The city had a temple built in honor of Diana, the goddess of fertility. She was also known as Artemis to the Greeks. The temple became one of the seven wonders of the ancient world.[3]

Paul worked in the area for three years, helping to establish the church. Following his departure, both Timothy and the apostle John carried on the work. Paul's aim in this letter is to bring the Ephesian church back in line with the Gospel's truth and create unity among its members. But, unfortunately, the converted Jews were inclined to be exclusive and separate themselves from Gentile believers, causing the church's division.[4]

---

[2] The Thompson Chain-Reference Bible, New International Version, Zondervan Bible Publishers, 1983.
[3] https://www.bibleplaces.com/ephesus/.
[4] https://www.history.com/topics/ancient-greece/ephesus.

First Draft Pick Chosen

EPHESIANS 1:3–14

We always used the same technique for dividing teams when the neighborhood kids gathered for baseball or whiffle ball. Someone would toss a baseball bat to another player. First, they would catch the bat as close to the end as they could. Then the person who threw the bat would set their hand above the receiver's hand. Next, they would alternate hand placement turns with each person, connecting the bottom of their hand to the top of the opponent's hand. The winner would be the one closest to the knob end. That person would then swing the bat back and forth three times. If they maintained their grip, then they were awarded the first pick. If not, the other person got the first pick.

The winner would then look over the available players and pick the best one. The other team captain would then select among the rest. This selection process continued until all who were left were the two worst players. I was usually one of these two players. The one selected next to last could feel like they weren't the worst in the batch.

I was usually the last one selected.

You see, during my years in youth sports, I played right field. Those who understand youth sports know that the preceding statement means I'm not that great of an athlete. Later in life, I would joke that the coaches in whatever sport I played had tremendous confidence in me. I reasoned this because they would put me in the game if we were thirty points ahead or thirty points behind in the waning moments of the game to hold the lead or cut the deficit. Lacking athletic skills allowed me to learn about God's gifts and abilities in other areas. Still, it did not make me feel any better about my participation in games during the formative years of my life.

From kindergarten through the first half of my seventh-grade year, the house I lived in had four bare spots in the front yard. No matter what Dad tried, grass would not grow there. The reason why was simple; we called them first base, second base, third base, and home plate. Our yard was the neighborhood baseball and whiffle ball field. Dad also put up a basketball goal by our driveway. Try as I might, I never developed the skill level to be more than the last person chosen.

When I got into junior high and high school physical education classes, I found the same team selection process. The coach designated a captain, and they selected teams from first to worst. During my freshman year, I realized the coaches had the classes perform the same sports currently in season. I supposed it was to find any hidden talent that had not tried out for the team. Not only was the selection process humiliating, but it got worse when the captain, an offensive lineman on the freshman team, would put me on the offensive line so he could play quarterback or wide receiver. Offensive linemen never get to touch the football in a real game or practice. They would make up for this during gym class. Defensive linemen are different in that they like their jobs in real games and gym class. My team lined me up as an offensive lineman against a defensive lineman twice my size and much more talented in the game. Somehow, I was supposed to stop this giant from getting to my quarterback without sacrificing my life and health. I always failed, which made the team selection process destined to make me the last selection for life but kept my mother happy that I wasn't injured or dead.

In my recreation leadership class, I teach about how organizers should select teams for recreational events. The textbook we use states that one of the worst ways of picking teams is by appointing a captain and choosing teams in front of everyone. The reason is simple; no one wants to be the last person chosen. I have had the pain of being chosen last in sports and the joy of being the first-round draft pick for projects. It feels better to be the first one selected.

Before you start feeling completely sorry for me, I wasn't the last one chosen in everything. When classes had to create a presentation and needed someone to stand in front of the class, I was the first one selected. If the assignment was for someone to be goofy and silly, teams would compete for me like prized free agents in professional sports where the first-round draft picks demand more attention and more money. I found my talent, niche, and gifts in being the silly person at the front.

In 1978, the National Basketball Association team, Boston Celtics, took advantage of a loophole whereby a team could draft a player after the student's class graduated. The team selected Larry Bird with the sixth pick of the first round, even though Bird had one more year of college eligibility, which he chose to use. Five teams drafted before the Celtics but decided not to risk that Bird would not get injured or that he would decide to sign with another team in the next year's draft. The Celtics took Bird on their belief that he would be one of the best in the game. They were correct in their summation.[5] It pains a lifelong Los Angeles Laker fan like myself to heap this much praise on a Boston player, but Mr. Bird makes a point of being chosen above the rest of the bunch perfectly.

When the apostle Paul wrote his cell call to the church in Ephesus, he wanted to make sure they knew where they fit in the team selection by God. "Even before he made the world, God loved us and chose us in Christ to be holy and without fault in his eyes" (Ephesians 1:4 NLT). In the continuing verses, Paul explains that God chose us in advance to adopt us and place us on His team, which gives Him great pleasure.

To further state the point, Paul explains in verse 11, "For he chose us in advance, and he makes everything work out according to his plan" (Ephesians 1:11 NLT). We weren't only a number one draft pick; God chose us long before we even knew there would be a team. God chose us before we chose Him. Like the Celtics, God knew we would

---

[5] https://www.quora.com/How-was-Larry-Bird-drafted-by-the-Boston-Celtics-in-1978–but-played-his-final-season-at-Indiana-State-in-1979.

be one of the best in the game of life. God chose us early, taking a chance we might be injured, knowing we would be one of the best.

There's a beauty about God choosing us with a first draft pick. Despite our flaws, failures, and foul-ups, God wants us on His team. In another letter to the believers in Rome, Paul wrote, "While we were yet sinners, Christ died for us" (Romans 5:8 KJV). God realizes that we can't be defensive linemen in gym class because some need to be clowns, musicians, or mathematicians. He designed you exactly how He wanted you, which is for you to be you. Or, as Dr. Seuss would put it, "Today you are you! That is truer than true. There is no one alive who is you-er than you!"[6]

In other words, you give God great pleasure when you are yourself and not trying to be something or someone that you're not. Paul even comments that he continued his prayers for the people of Ephesus while remaining in a thankful spirit for knowing them.

In this particular cell call, Paul reminded the people of Ephesus that they were here for a reason. God chose them to carry out His work through them. No need to be ashamed of what your gifts are or are not. Take the skills, talents, and abilities God gave you and perform them for His glory and His pleasure. Paul even offers to pray for those in Ephesus that they would experience the hope and power that comes with being one of God's chosen. Somehow, I can imagine Jesus is in heaven, offering the same prayer for you today.

Just imagine yourself at the draft selection event where the league commissioner says, "God, the first pick of the draft is yours."

Without hesitation, God says, "With my number one draft pick, I choose _____ [fill in your name here] because 'Today you are you! That is truer than true. There is no one alive who is you-er than you!'"[7]

Congratulations! You're God's number one draft pick!

---

[6] *Happy Birthday to You!* by Dr. Seuss | PenguinRandomHouse.com."
[7] Dr. Seuss.

Prayers Are Paul's Specific Ocean for Ephesian Friends

Ephesians 1:15–23

One of the joys I've received from being active on social media is the number of people willing to point out grammatical errors. I would be like Paul when it comes to grammar because I am the "chief of sinners." I'm bad enough that I purchased a grammar correction web service to assist me in writing blogs and books. The beauty of this service is that it will tell me that I used the wrong word, misspelled a word, or wrote passively. I'm incredibly guilty of writing passively. I get pretty aggressive about my passive writing.

I recommended this service to the editorial board of the Association of Church Sports and Recreation Ministries publishing service and, in the recommendation, misspelled the word *grammar*. One of the board members pointed out that I should have used the service before sending the email. The editor for my first book told me it would take some extra effort to "clean up my grammar." I asked him if it was that bad. He said, "Let's just say there's a difference between proper English and hillbilly English."

I understood completely. I told my college English 101 professor that I wrote as I spoke. He said, "That's a good thing." Then I spoke, and he said he understood my difficulty in writing.

The title of this part of Paul's cell call is one of those examples pointed out by the grammar police on social media. Of note, using specific rather than pacific. Or phrases like "all intents and purposes"

A CELL CALL FROM PAUL

instead of "all intensive purposes." Finally, the calling out of the improper use of they're, their, and there. In the case of this chapter, the "specific" is purposeful, as Paul lets his Ephesian friends know he is praying for them in specific ways. The definition of *specific* is "precise or particular."[8] Pacific, which is an ocean, is defined as seventy million square miles.[9] The difference between the two definitions is enormous. Specific prayers are precise and particular. Pacific prayers cover a lot of ground.

I've been guilty of offering "Pacific" prayers. I've developed the "God bless all the missionaries" prayer into an art form. When I was on church staff at Germantown Baptist in the Memphis, Tennessee, area, we created a four-sided prayer wall in our main lobby. The purpose of the wall was to have four people, one for each wall, praying twenty-four hours a day. The church was large enough to fill all the time slots. My time started at 11:00 p.m. on Wednesdays. I would get a call from the 10:00 p.m. person to get me started. When I completed my hour, I would call the midnight person for that day. I'm ashamed to admit many of my prayers ended up being more of a roll call of people on my list than it was a specific prayer for people. My prayers might go like this: "God help Sam. God help my wife. God be with my children. God bless our ministry." And so on. While I believe God hears any prayer, in some cases praying specifically, not *pacifically*, is helpful.

My mother shared a specific prayer she had for me during my youth and young adult years. She sensed in me a very unhealthy sense of pride. I wouldn't ask for help no matter what the circumstances. One time, she observed me arguing with a couple who knew I was going into the ministry and were trying to give me something as a love offering. The envelope went back and forth between us, with the argument going like this: "We want you to have this," and "You don't need to do this." The couple finally gave up, and I was without the gift. I was nineteen years old at the time, and I think she wanted to

---

[8] https://www.dictionary.com/browse/specific.
[9] https://www.dictionary.com/browse/pacific-ocean.

sit me in the corner as if I were still seven years old. Because of this pride, her prayer was that God would put people in my life who would keep me humble. At one point, I requested that she stop praying the humility-giver prayers, as that seemed to be all God was placing in my life! If you know some of the people who remain in my life, you'll know Mom has not stopped praying her specific prayer for me.

As any expectant father, I prayed "pacifically" for the health and well-being of each of my children. My prayer immediately became specific when the doctors diagnosed heart trouble in the first little one. Throughout the early years with my three sons, I prayed that God would make them more accomplished and better men than me. God answered that specific prayer, as all three got to that point and surpassed me by their twelfth birthday. When the boys or their mom were sick, I remember praying specifically for God to ease their pain and let me have it instead.

When I saw the two movies *Won't You Be My Neighbor* and *It's a Beautiful Day in the Neighborhood*, I was intrigued by the prayer habits of Mr. Rogers. My third son and the wife of my first son have done in-depth studies into the life of Mr. Rogers and how he helped shape an entire generation. Jan White, writing the article "Mister Rogers' Life of Prayer for His Neighborhood," shared information about his prayer life from the book *The Simple Faith of Mister Rogers* by Amy Hollingsworth. In her book, she describes Mister Rogers as a man of prayer. She writes that his daily routine began at 5:00 a.m. with prayer, reflection, and Bible reading. "Each morning he prayed for his family and friends by name … The prayers continued into his workday."[10]

Far too often, I tend to formalize prayer too much. I get mad at myself when I find I'm just reading off a list to God, so, instead, I try to pray as if I were doing so in front of the church. I use my teaching voice as I talk to God. I find myself using my teaching voice when I'm teaching, which I suppose would be normal, other than it's

---

[10] https://www.andalusiastarnews.com/2019/11/15/mister-rogers-life-of-prayer-for-his-neighborhood/.

nothing like my normal voice. It becomes comical when a student asks a question, and I respond with a normal voice. Once I answer the question, I go back into the teaching voice mode. I'm grateful God listens to whatever voice I use because far too many students ignore the teaching voice.

In reality, prayer is having a conversation with God. My friends will tell you there's nothing formal about my normal conversations. I don't generally discuss work, sports, or what is going on in the world with a teacher voice. My friends and I speak specifically about those topics. I should do the same when I speak with God. Paul, who wrote to another church about "never stop praying" (1 Thessalonians 5:17 NLT), tells his Ephesian friends that he prays for them constantly.

Paul's first specific prayer was for God to give spiritual wisdom and insight so his friends could grow in their knowledge of God. Wisdom and insight are specific, especially in light of the false teaching occurring in the Ephesian church. It's easy to fall for things that sound true but are not true. For example, I thought the statement "God helps those who help themselves" was in the Bible for the longest time. However, wisdom and insight finally kicked in when a friend challenged me to find it in the scriptures.

Paul also prayed for his friends to be flooded with light to understand God's calling in their lives to gain His glorious inheritance. The people of Ephesus, like me, forgot who they were in Christ. We are more than "saved sinners." We are brothers and sisters of Jesus, making us eligible to be God's rich and glorious inheritance.

Finally, Paul prayed that his friends would know and comprehend the tremendous power of God, which raised Jesus from the dead. The power of God has authority over any authority, power, or leader in this world. This reminder would be beneficial in the time of Roman rule. It's not a bad reminder to those of us living in our current culture. No matter how powerful the Romans appeared on earth, there is a heavenly power we know personally to which Rome eventually must answer. The governments of the world today are still in the same place as the Romans were then. So, whether one is

DAVID WADDELL

Republican, Democrat, independent, libertarian, labor, conservative, liberal, socialist, or communist, we are all under God's power.

Part of this specific prayer was so the Ephesians would know that all of Christ's authority is for the church and is made complete in our relationship with Christ. The pacific love of Christ is specifically for each of us. That's a statement even the grammar police would accept!

You're Not That Bad

EPHESIANS 2:1–10

Do you ever have the hopeless feeling that you're so bad there's no way God could love you? Do you compare yourself to others and believe no one could ever be as evil as you might be? I've felt that way several times in my life. Let me share one in particular during a visit with my counselor years ago.

I sat on the couch as he took his customary seat in a rocking chair. There was a clock that sat on a table next to him. The clock was always twenty minutes ahead of the actual time. All around the walls of the room were shelves of books. During our session, he would often get up from the chair, walk directly to one shelf, and pull off a book that had a quote or a story that would help me get through the issues of that day.

He was my therapist. I started seeing him at the request of my pastor, church, and the restoration team I was assigned after I confessed to some hidden sin in my life. The sin created the necessity for me to resign as the church's recreation pastor. Still, the pastor and the leadership team in the church desired to see healing rather than hurt in establishing my connection with a counselor at the church's expense. My counselor was a few years older and was a church member where I had just resigned. He had long gray hair matched by a long gray beard. He was soft-spoken and quite adept at assisting me in finding the answers rather than prescribing what I should do.

In those first few meetings, I began to open up and share how I ended up so deep in sinful choices. I explained the circumstances that placed me in a position where I was vulnerable to temptation. I shared how shame had become such a part of my life. Shame is an ugly part of life. I told the counselor that I was hiding sin in my life during my twenty-plus years of ministry leadership in churches. The shame of this sin would play games in my head about how I was unworthy to serve God. The same shame would also convince me to remain quiet to keep my life looking good. The shame would lie that I was helping my marriage survive and allowing me to serve others better in ministry. The shame of my actions would also inspire me to create new programs in the recreation ministry of the church designed to tell more people about Jesus. These actions convinced me that all was well in my life. I just had to keep hiding the sin and shame.

Then, the discovery of sin and shame came. Deleted emails somehow reappeared in my account, and, bit by bit, I confessed all of the sins I was hiding. An eventual divorce, loss of respect from my sons, and resignation from ministry leadership made me feel more shame than before. I have this war going on in my heart. Part of me seeks out sinful desires, and part of me wants to run as hard as I can away from them. The war wages even harder when I am not honest about my struggles and attempt to show others that I have life figured out and have all my stuff together.

In one session, I felt worse about what I had done to my wife and family, along with the church. I told my counselor that I didn't feel worthy of the love of Jesus. My sin was too harsh for forgiveness. This wise counselor leaned back in his rocking chair and knew precisely how to communicate with me. He said, "Yes, I suppose Jesus's death paid for everyone's sin except yours."

Sarcasm was not his usual mode of communication, but he knew it would catch my attention and penetrate my heart more than an argument or statement of faith. Even today, when shame tries to remind me of my worthlessness, the words of this counselor play in my head. I was dead in my sin and have been made alive again in Christ.

When Paul made his cell call to the church in Ephesus, he made sure to remind them of the same truth—that Jesus has brought them out of a life of disobedience into a life of being one with Christ. He acknowledges in verse 4, "we were dead because of our sins." None of us were better than the rest of us, and even the best of us were not better than any of the rest of us. Furthermore, Paul tells the Ephesians that they were raised from the dead with Christ by God's grace and saved by His grace.

The people to which Paul sent this cell call were Gentiles or non-Jews. Before everyone heard the Gospel, many "us and them" segregations took place in this culture. It doesn't appear that much has changed in the world since Paul made this cell call. Part of the Jewish culture attempted to shame the Gentiles for not being the original chosen people of God. The lifestyle of many Gentiles demonstrated how far away they were from God's level of holiness commanded by scripture, which led the Jews of that time to feel superior to the Gentiles. Some even felt Gentiles should go through the process of circumcision first and then be allowed into Christ's church. The Ephesians found more of what was different in each other than that which they had in common. In other words, Jesus's death was good enough for everyone except them.

This "us and them" message Paul shared is still a relevant cell call for us today. God's love is not restricted to any of the differences we find in people today. Instead, God loves all and desires a relationship with everyone, despite differences in our culture's other divisive aspects of life.

Paul takes the Ephesians back to the basics and the fundamentals of the faith to make his point. I read that when John Wooden coached the University of California at Los Angeles (UCLA), he would take All-American high school athletes, and the first thing he would do was teach them how to put on their socks and shoes.[11] Wooden knew that blisters would develop if a player incorrectly put on their socks and shoes, causing that player to sit on the bench. It was his way of going back to the basics and the fundamentals of the game. Paul takes the Ephesians back to the basics of grace. In verse 8, he states, "God

---

[11] (http://www.johnsadowsky.com/a-tale-of-socks-and-shoes/).

saved you by his grace when you believed. And you can't take credit for this: it is a gift from God" (Ephesians 2:8 NLT).

Salvation is not something that is a birthright or solely for one people group. Paul calls us all "God's masterpiece" in that He created us to be new in Christ Jesus (Ephesians 2:9-10). The death and resurrection of Jesus did pay the price for everyone. Even me.

Paul is precise in teaching the Ephesians that the death and resurrection of Christ brought the two very different people groups together into one body by one faith through one Spirit. In another letter Paul wrote to the church in Galatia, he said, "There is no longer Jew or Gentile, slave or free, male and female. For you are all one in Christ Jesus" (Galatians 3:28 NLT).

Christ destroyed the wall of hostility that separates us. The death and resurrection of Jesus put us in unity with all believers. We are more alike than we are different. Paul says this coming together is being a part of His house. It's as if a building was being built and joined together by Christ, the cornerstone. Therefore, all of us have a part in the dwelling place where God lives by His Spirit.

It would appear that Christ's death was good enough for even my sin and your sin. See, you're not as bad as you thought. And I'm not even saying that sarcastically!

The More We Get Together

Ephesians 2:11-22

Since I met Lewis in 1998, he's been one of my best friends and most incredible supporters. Originally from New York, he moved to Alabama as a child and has been southern ever since. My first meeting with him was over youth baseball at our church. He told me I was doing something wrong and it would be better to do it another way, which he pointed out. It ended up that he was right.

We worked together a few years later as he opened a little café in the church's recreation center. He created a breakfast for me, known as the cholesterol special. It was two fried eggs, cooked over-easy, set on two heavily buttered pieces of toast. When sin in my life was exposed and I resigned from my position in the church, Lewis served on my accountability team. I continued to make a weekly visit for the cholesterol special before working at my new job.

When I accepted the position at the University of Mississippi, he and I initiated a tradition of us attending the Ole Miss–Auburn football game each year. But, unfortunately, he celebrates more than I do with the outcomes of those games.

When I took on the volunteer position of executive director of the Association of Church Sports and Recreation Ministries (CSRM), the organization needed some guidance. So, I sought Lewis out to serve on our board. His leading retail organizations and his business-savvy leadership style helped me form a plan for the association.

Lewis, as I see it, has only one flaw. He's a fan of the New York Yankees. Let me explain. From my childhood, I have learned to despise the New York Yankees. My maternal grandfather hated them with a passion. For three years, 1976–1978, my father had World Series tickets for our family sitting on his desk at home. Each of those three years, we could not use them because the dreaded New York Yankees beat my beloved Kansas City Royals.

So, how is it he is one of my best friends? I'll explain later in this chapter.

I stood next to the CSRM booth as everyone prepared for an international sports and recreation ministry workshop. Then the representative from BSN Sports left his booth and approached me. He was wearing a Mississippi State University Bulldog shirt, and I had on an Ole Miss shirt. As he came to me, he said, "I guess we are not supposed to like each other?"

These two schools have a rivalry that would make the Hatfields and McCoys look like a church picnic. There is an incredible amount of hatred, disrespect, and wishing the other school would lose. It's bad enough that if an athlete from either school gets in trouble with the law, some fans will celebrate their demise. Thankfully, this man and I are not that steeped in the rivalry. We both laughed at his statement and introduced ourselves to each other. Richard has become a great friend and confidant to me. Our enjoyment of cheering for our respective schools does not hinder our friendship. More on that later.

In the summer of 2020, a declaration announced that certain outdoor activities could occur during the coronavirus pandemic. My church decided to conduct outdoor worship services in addition to the online presence. I chose to attend and set my lawn chair up socially distant from everyone else. My mask, made by my sister-in-law, Joy, has the Kansas City Chiefs logo on it. I put it over my mouth as a man approached me. It was Joey, our new next generation pastor. We talked briefly, and then he confessed, "I'm a Raiders fan in football."

It was a defining moment for me. As a Kansas City Chiefs fan, we root for two teams—the Chiefs and whoever plays the Raiders. But I realized faith is more important than football, and we have become good friends. I even had to admit that his baby daughter looked fabulous while wearing a Raiders jersey. I do wonder, however, how Proverbs 22:6, "Direct your children on the right path, and when they are older, they will not leave it" (NLT), applies to Yankees and Raiders fans. I suppose I hope the children would grow out of it.

It's easy to find the division with people. In this story, I relate the difference of following rival sports teams. However, the division isn't just about teams and games. Differences today are pointed out in our ethnicity, racial background, political beliefs, and many other items. I fear we spend more time trying to find out how we are different rather than celebrating similarities.

I make it a point to keep my political leanings to myself. Political beliefs are so passionate that they often create difficulties in friendships. The politics aren't just in who we vote for either. Sometimes it's stands we take in churches over direction or decisions. The lines were evident when the Southern Baptists dealt with some of their issues in the latter part of the twentieth century. You had to be on one side or the other. Churches, families, and friends split on the issue. A friend asked me where I stood on the issues, and I told her I sat on the fence right in the middle. She pointed out I had to take one side or the other, and I commented that not only was I sitting on the fence, but I had a pillow to keep the chain-link wire from poking me too hard on my backside.

So, let's address the issue of making friends with those I can't entirely agree with team fandom, politics, or other differences. In this cell call to the Ephesians, Paul reminds them that Christ has united all people together. It would appear that there was still an unsettled feeling about how Gentiles should become Christians in the minds of some Jews. The rift between Jews and Gentiles was as old as the founding of the nation in Abraham. The separation continues to this day in some parts of the world.

Paul points out that Jews and Gentiles have become one in Jesus. He reminds the Gentiles that they were once "outsiders" and called "uncircumcised heathens." Paul also puts the Jews in their place with his follow-up comment that circumcision affected their bodies but not their hearts.

The key to Paul's defense of both Jew and Gentile is in verse 14, "For Christ himself has brought peace to us. He united Jews and Gentiles into one people when, in his own body on the cross, he broke down the wall of hostility that separated us" (NLT). Later, in verse 16, Paul claims that Jesus put the hostility wall to death through His death. Paul, who wrote to the church in Corinth that their body was the temple of the Holy Spirit, made a similar point to the Ephesians. He told the church that, together, Jews and Gentiles are Jesus's house, where Jesus is the cornerstone and the apostles and prophets have laid the foundation. We are all a dwelling place where God lives.

One of the songs I remember from my years working in our church's camping ministry is the song "The More We Get Together." The lyrics will give you an idea of why I named this part of *A Cell Call from Paul* by that title.

> The more we get together
> Together, together
> The more we get together
> The happier we'll be
>
> 'Cause your friends are my friends
> And my friends are your friends.[12]

Through His death, Christ made it where the more we get together with people with whom we have differences of thoughts, beliefs, and actions, the more we see our similarities in being a part of God's family. This sense of unity is why I can worship with a Raiders fan, claim a Yankees fan as a best friend, and partner in ministry with a Mississippi State Bulldog. Or why I can sit calmly with a Republican or a Democrat and why I can love both sides of a church fight or split. All of this is because Jesus destroyed the hostility between us and made us one.

Let's get together soon!

---

[12] https://www.kidsongs.com/lyrics/the-more-we-get-together.html.

You Guys, Youins, and All Y'all

Ephesians 3:1–13

I have noticed across our world that there are various accents and unique ways of talking. Local slang and derivatives of words play into forms of communication that can label where one lives or grew up. For example, in describing other people, I have had others referred to as "you guys, youins," and "y'all." A "you guys" places someone from the northeast, and the "youins" is popular among many hillbilly areas. One "y'all" out of my mouth, and people know I reside in the southern part of the United States. I picked up the "y'all" verbiage when I served at First Baptist Church in Natchez, Mississippi. It was a "when in Rome, do as the Romans" moment. I took the senior adults on a northeast tour one of the years, stopping in New York City. After dinner, I got on the elevator to go up to my hotel room when I saw a couple approaching. I held the door open and said, "Y'all, c'mon!"

The couple stopped in their tracks, smiled, and asked me to repeat myself. They were intrigued by the southern drawl and the use of the word *y'all*. During my time in Natchez, I also discovered the plural of *y'all* is *all y'all*.

I saw this communication feature played out when several Missouri churches combined forces to assist a church-planting effort in the London suburb of Tilbury. The United Kingdom is where you might hear someone say "yous" or "ye." They don't have a detour in the road; they have a diversion. They don't eat cookies; they have biscuits. I met a man with the last name spelled "Doyle," which he pronounced "dial."

I met Mr. Doyle (pronounced dial) when I was part of an exploratory journey with several church leaders in the spring of 1994. I saw the initial journey as an excellent opportunity to see what my church could do to help with the project. I also recognized it was a trip to the United Kingdom, a place I had long desired to visit. So, after various meetings over two days, the group took one day to tour popular spots in London.

After one of the days of meetings, the group went to a local pub for dinner. The pub featured two dinner options. I recall one option was shepherd pie, which I had always wanted to try. I don't remember the other choice except that it offered a side of Yorkshire pudding. I asked the server if it was possible to have "y'all" serve me the shepherd pie and the Yorkshire pudding for an additional fee. After much reluctance on his part and begging on mine, the server, recognizing my tourist accent as not belonging to someone from London, agreed to arrange for me to receive both items.

The meal arrived, and the shepherd pie, some green peas, and a biscuit-looking thing sitting on top of the pie were on the plate. Being a lover of good food, I ate every bit of food on my plate. The server came to the table to see if we needed anything else. I shared with him that I had not received my Yorkshire pudding yet. He said that I had. I argued with him and said, "I think I'd remember what I just ate for dinner."

The server became more and more adamant that I had received everything I ordered. Finally, I decided to explain that all I had on my plate was the pie, the peas, and the biscuit-looking thing. To this, the server mimicked my accent and said, "Y'all, that biscuit-looking thing was the Yorkshire pudding."

I should be glad he knew that biscuit-looking thing wasn't a cookie-looking thing. My face turned red with embarrassment as I turned to a table where some locals were sitting. I said, "Can y'all tell I'm not from here?"

One of them smiled back, shook one hand back and forth as if it were pivoting off the wrist, and said, "Hmm, not so much."

It was nice of the gentleman to diminish my embarrassment and offer a small glimpse of hope that I belonged there. The primary feeling of belonging is quite remarkable. So, one feels comfortable when y'all, youins, yous, ye, and you guys can experience connection.

It was between 1987 and 1992 that I worked at a church in Natchez, Mississippi. The area was known as the Deep South. While everyone was a *y'all* in this town, some held onto old views that segregated people into specific groups. One day, a gentleman, who had observed African Americans playing lunch basketball with me, approached me in my office and wanted to ask me a question. I sensed, after the question, that he was looking for a fight more than information. His question was, "What would you do if one of those African American basketball players tried to join our church?"

I responded, "I would greet him, shake his hand, and expect him to start tithing."

He didn't take to my offering humor and pressed the notion that the person might want to cause trouble. I refuted him by pointing out far better ways to cause problems than to join our church. "In fact," I continued, "the only trouble he or she would cause would be from people that won't accept him or her as Jesus would." In other words, any person can become a part of y'all, youins, yous, ye, and you guys in the church. The church should be the one place where all y'all, youins, yous, ye, and you guys are all welcome without question. Instead, we base our decisions on who will be y'all, youins, yous, ye, and you guys by whether they dress correctly, look hygienic, or don't have visible tattoos. Other people differentiate y'all, youins, yous, ye, and you guys by political beliefs, life choices, and educational or financial status. The church I attend in Oxford, Mississippi, has a sign at the front entrance that says, "No one is more welcome here than you." We don't care if you refer to us as y'all, youins, yous, ye, or you guys; as long as you show up, you are welcome.

One of the significant skirmishes in the early church was whether Gentiles had to become Jews before belonging to Christ's church. The Jews tried to separate themselves from others who were a part of y'all, youins, yous, ye, and you guys. The feeling of many Jews was that Gentiles should take on the ritual of becoming a Jew first. This ritual included the Abrahamic tradition of circumcision, which cut away the foreskin on the male genitalia. Just a side note that, in my opinion, circumcision would make the new member's class in church a problematic proposition. The discussion made many Gentiles feel they didn't belong in the same faith as those y'all, youins, yous, ye, and you guys Jewish believers. Then again, this ritual is not the same as wearing a tattoo in plain sight.

In numerous discussions and his cell call to the Ephesians, Paul brought believers back to the basics of faith in Christ. He pointed out that God not only invites the Gentiles to become y'all, youins, yous, ye, and you guys as they are, but also God has called him to be a proclaimer of the Gospel to the Gentiles. What is now known as the third chapter of his cell call, Paul states, "I, Paul, a prisoner of Christ Jesus for the benefit of you Gentiles ... assuming, by the way, that you know God gave me the special responsibility of extending his grace to you Gentiles" (Ephesians 3:1-2 NLT). Depending on where you reside, the interpretation could be, "I, Paul, a prisoner of Christ Jesus for the benefit of y'all, youins, yous, ye, and you guys."

In his infinite wisdom, Paul points out that God invited all y'all, youins, yous, ye, and you guys to be a part of His family to display His wisdom and grace to all sorts of rulers and authorities. So even while Paul was in this Roman prison, he was busy sharing Christ with all of y'all, youins, yous, ye, and you guys around Rome.

Paul closes out this part of his cell call reminding the Ephesians and us that because God has included y'all, youins, yous, ye, and you guys in His family, we can go to His presence in confidence and boldness. Paul refers to his personal trials and sufferings but states he does it for the cause of Christ. In that, he honors all of y'all, youins, yous, ye, and you guys in the Ephesian church by his suffering.

Like Paul and the Ephesians, I should not judge a person by any labels this world places on them. I remember the scene in the movie *Remember the Titans* where a Caucasian Gerry Bertier lay injured in bed from an automobile accident. An African American teammate, Julius Campbell, enters the room and is told visitation is for family only. Gary says to the nurse, "Alice, are you blind? Don't you see the family resemblance? That's my brother."[13]

May y'all, youins, yous, ye, and you guys all start seeing each other by the only label needed, that being our brother and sister in Christ.

---

[13] https://www.imdb.com/title/tt0210945/characters/nm0085994.

Often Is Heard an Encouraging Word

EPHESIANS 3:14–21

Throughout my life, I have taken three different tests on numerous occasions. One of those deals with career paths. When I complete these assessments, the results are that I should go into ministry, teaching, or work with people in another capacity. When I refer to these exams to my students at the University of Mississippi, I caution them to review the findings against their passions, talents, and interests. If the career assessment doesn't match your perceived calling, I recommend taking another assessment when other stresses may not influence the outcome. I give the students an example of when I was bothered by some people I worked with in a church and took an online career assessment that told me I should work in some private cubicle. I knew this was a bogus response due to the stress I had with certain people. However, there's no way I'd maintain sanity staying entirely away from people. The pandemic of 2020 has confirmed this aspect of my life.

The second type of exam is the personality test. People who know me will not be surprised that I always fall high on the extraverted scale. I'm the person who wants to be in front of the crowd. Early in my ministry career, I attempted my luck at being a Christian comedian. I spoke to several churches at banquets and retreats with a comical look at being a Christian. I confess to my students that I attempted the standup comic career on a part-time basis. When

I realized that particular career path wouldn't work out, I started teaching. Unfortunately, too many students still think I'm a joke!

When I'm at conferences, and we have a small group discussion, I'm the one who volunteers to share our findings with the entire group. An example of my outgoing nature occurred in my junior year of high school in English class. We were divided into groups and tasked with writing a commercial. Roberta, Mike, Linda, and I were assigned together in the group. We decided to write a commercial like the late-night ones for used-car sales. My nickname in high school was Pierre, so we named the used-car salesman Pierre Pepe Le Pew. I volunteered to take the performance lead and stood in front of the class. I fast-talked my way, like any good late-night used-car salesman, through various heaps of junk that were for sale on my car lot.

The third type of test is the spiritual gift inventory. This test is similar to the two previous exams where it gives scenarios or situations, and you respond how you would deal with each of those. Again, those who know me would not be surprised that I consistently score high on the gift of encouragement. I get such joy out of encouraging others. When a friend thanks me or appreciates me practicing my gift, I quickly let them know we possess a great combination of me with the gift of encouragement and the other person with so much talent and ability to encourage.

In the leadership class I instruct with sports and recreation majors, I tell them that encouragement is one of the keys to success. I encourage them to find what their team or staff is doing right and praise them for it. A culture of encouragement allows the team to function and try new things. Encouragement breeds growth in a person.

I received a lot of encouragement growing up. I think that helped shape and form the gift that God gave me. One of my memories from youth sports was from a very encouraging man who coached our church's baseball team. As I have stated before, I played the position of right field, which tells people the athletic prowess I didn't possess. In one game, the batter hit the ball toward me in right field, and I made the classic outfielder mistake by running in for the pop-up, only to see it sail over my head. I turned and ran to get the ball and throw it back to the infield. I hustled enough that I held what should have been a fly out into a triple.

After we got the third out and returned to our bench, our coach, Ed Christian, congratulated me on my fantastic hustle to chase down the ball and hold the batter to a triple. As a ten-year-old boy, I knew I fouled the play, yet Coach Christian wanted to find the good in me and proclaim it out loud for the team to hear. That play was over fifty years ago, and I still remember the encouragement to this day. It was people like Ed Christian who taught me the power of an encouraging word.

Paul spent some of his cell call to the Ephesian church offering them encouraging words. Paul, like me, had a great teacher for this supportive trait. For years, his missionary partner was Barnabas, whose nickname was the Son of Encouragement. After Paul's miraculous salvation on the road to Damascus, the early church was suspicious of meeting with the former persecutor of Christians. Barnabas stepped in and shared Paul's story and how he had preached Jesus in Damascus. It was Barnabas's encouragement that allowed Paul to step into his ministry role (Acts 9:26–27).

Paul's encouragement to the Ephesians in this part of his cell call included his hopes and prayers for his friends. Paul spoke of unlimited resources that were available from God, which would empower their inner strength. He spoke of their hearts as being the home of Christ. He talked about how their roots would grow deep in God's love. This last one has a particular meaning for me. The church I attend in Oxford is named "The Orchard." The mantra or motto for the church is "Growing Deep—Branching Out." The further rooted the Ephesians got into God's Word and His love, the more they could have the power to understand His work in their lives.

Later in the cell call, he tells the Ephesians that they not only belong in God's family but that they also get an equal share of God's inheritance for His children. That's pretty encouraging, right? Paul further explains that God's belonging and love for us is wide, long, high, and deep. Growing up, we sang a song titled "Deep and Wide" about God's overflowing fountain. The lyrics were as follows:

> Deep and wide, deep and wide
> There's a fountain flowing deep and wide.
> Deep and wide, deep and wide
> There's a fountain flowing deep and wide.[14]

Of course, hand motions demonstrated depth by holding one hand vertically over the other, and the hands showed wide with similar horizontal motions. So when we sang the second time around, the fun part of the song was we'd drop the word *deep* and make an "mmph" sound while continuing to make the hand gestures. On the third go-around, *wide* followed the same silent approach, with hand gestures and an "mmph," which would create the following song:

> Mmph and mmph, mmph and mmph
> There's a fountain flowing mmph and mmph.
> Mmph and mmph, mmph and mmph
> There's a fountain flowing mmph and mmph.

When one realizes how deep, broad, far, wide, ample, far-reaching, spacious, high, immense, huge, long, and immeasurable God's love is, we find the greatest sense of encouragement. Substituting mmph and mmph doesn't change the nature of God's love, mercy, and grace for us. As I've heard numerous pastors proclaim, "There is nothing we can do that will make God love us more, and nothing we can do, regardless of how evil it may be, would make God love us less."

Paul tells his Ephesian friends that they can accomplish much more than they might think or ask through God's love. His cell call to us will affirm the same accomplishment.

That's the kind of mmph and mmph love we all need. I find that fact quite encouraging.

---

[14] http://jessejoyner.com/who-wrote-the-deep-and-wide-song/.

One for All and All for One

EPHESIANS 4:1–16

It's weird how the memory calls up certain things from our past. I don't remember the plot, title, or storyline, but an old *Three Stooges* episode had the threesome playing the three musketeers. At a critical point in the skit, the three placed their swords on top of each other and then quoted the famous musketeer line, one stooge at a time, with a notable exception:

> Moe: "All for one!"
> Larry: "One for all!"
> Curly: "Every man for himself!"

At that point, the stooges took off running in different directions, with Curly making his "whoop, whoop, whoop" sound. The stooges felt unified until the first danger arose. Then they suddenly had their individual agendas, that being personal safety.

Keeping the team together in a spirit of unity has long been a struggle for teachers, coaches, and pastors. Part of the human spirit causes us to desire our way, our agenda, and our conclusions. In addition, human design wants personal attention and notoriety. It takes a mighty swallow to get rid of the pride and perform for the best of the team.

Charley Rosen tells the story of the 1969 National Basketball Association championship final where two people on a team decided to play to their egos rather than the team's success. Wilt Chamberlain, center on the Los Angeles Lakers, committed his fifth foul late in the third quarter. If he received one more infraction, it would disqualify him for the remainder of the game. Up to that point, Chamberlain was proud of his record, having never fouled out of a game. So, midway through the final quarter, the coach, Butch van Breda Kolff, wanted to put him back in the game. Chamberlain refused and complained of a sore knee.

Later, near the end of the game, Chamberlain told Breda Kolff he was ready to go back in, and the coach, determined to win without his egotistical star, told him to go back to the bench and sit. The Boston Celtics eventually won the game. A personal goal that became more important to the player and the coach's ego may have prevented eventual team success.[15]

Things don't work as well without unity of mission and spirit. It's the same in the church. One for all and all for one only works if it's not every man for himself.

Paul often referred to the church as the "body of Christ." It's not hard to recognize how the body works. The brain sends a signal, and the different parts obediently comply. Yet there is often rebellion and the inability to work as a team, even in the body. As a child, I remember a comedy routine where the comedian told the story of the body communicating with itself. He spoke of how cocky and arrogant the brain can be in the body by using the account of walking through a dark room.

As a person walks through the room, the eyes ask the hand to turn on the lights. The brain, thinking it remembers where everything is, confidently says no. The comedian points out that the toes are screaming and desperately begging for the hand to turn on the lights.

This walking-in-the-dark situation happened to my former wife on one family vacation. She woke in the middle of the night in a hotel room to make her way to the bathroom. She didn't want to turn on the lights and wake up the kids, so she tried to make it through the

---

[15] Charley Rosen, *The Pivotal Season: How the 1971–1972 Lakers Changed the NBA.*

room. Unfortunately, her big toe met the leg of a table, she screamed in pain, and the waking of the kids she desperately wanted to avoid happened anyway. The following day, she limped around on the heel of the affected foot until we could get to an emergency room, where the physician told her she broke her big toe. The rest of the vacation for her was on crutches.

Having experienced broken bones in each foot, I know it affects how everything else works in the body. Also, I have a condition that affects my feet and legs, requiring other muscles to compensate for the disorder. I feel the effect on the knees and hips as they compensate when walking with the impact of that condition. The same principle applies when any part of the body doesn't work. Other parts have to kick in to make up the difference. The body doesn't work as well without unity of purpose. I've heard the Greek word used in this letter for unity, which means the mending of bones, which happened with a broken toe or the two outer metatarsals in my feet. When I broke the outer metatarsal on my left foot, the doctor had to put a screw in the foot to help the mending of the bones. As he removed the cast, I asked him if I could play the piano after removing the cast. He replied in the affirmative that I could. I said, "Good. I've always wanted to be able to play."

He paused from the cast removal, stared me straight in the eyes, and then went back to the work of taking off the cast. It was one of those timing jokes where I enjoyed it, but the recipient did not. The bones in my foot got back together for the sake of the body. It's the same in the church. One for all and all for one only works if it's not every man for himself.

Paul describes how the body works in the fourth chapter of his cell call to Ephesus. "Always be humble and gentle. Be patient with each other, making allowances for each other's faults because of your love. Make every effort to keep yourselves united in the Spirit, binding yourselves together with peace. For there is one body and one Spirit" (Ephesians 4:2–4a NLT).

When I think of the body at work, it reminds me of one of the more enjoyable children's songs I sang as a part of recreation ministry in churches: the spiritual "Dem Bones" by James Weldon Johnson. Here are a few of the lyrics that describe how everything is connected:

> Well, your toe bone connected to your foot bone
> Your foot bone connected to your heel bone
> Your heel bone connected to your ankle bone

The song continues with its obvious connection.

> Your backbone connected to your shoulder bone
> Your shoulder bone connected to your neck bone
> Your neck bone connected to your head bone
> I hear the word from the Lord![16]

During my time on staff at Germantown Baptist Church, we had a body diagram that we used to describe what a follower of Christ would resemble. It featured the mind of Christ, a heart of worship, a hand of connection to others, a hand that gives to others, a leg of ministry, and a leg of missions and evangelism. A relationship with Christ meant activity and growth in each area. Multiply this out by the number of people in one's church or the overall church, and you have an influential body of Christ in a community.

I love the way the body works. If one particular part is hurting, the other parts kick in extra to assist. I've read that people who are sight impaired develop their other senses more deeply than those with sight. I had a doctor who wanted to fix my feet disorder by clipping the nerve on the little toe. My parents refused, as the little toes provide much balance for the body.

In the same way the little toe is essential to the body, so are all the people with their various gifts in the body of Christ. Paul says in verse 7, "However, he has given each one of us a special gift through the generosity of Christ." Later in the cell call, he describes them. "Now these are the gifts Christ gave the church; the apostles, the prophets,

---

[16] Dry Bones lyrics © Leeds Music Corp, Essex Music International Inc. Universal-on-Backstreet Music, JEC Publishing Corp, CRML LTD.

the evangelists, and the pastor and teachers. Their responsibility is to equip God's people to do his work and build up the church, the body of Christ" (Ephesians 4:11-12 NLT).

I'm not sure which of those gifts the little toe would represent in the body of Christ. But I imagine anyone doing something for the church that the people don't usually recognize could be the little toe gifts at work. So, if your work doesn't get the glamor, take pride in the balance you quietly provide the body of Christ. You're far more vital than you may ever realize.

If we all use our gifts to build up the church and do so with humility, gentleness, and in the spirit of peace, we will be ready, unlike the three stooges, to say, "All for one and one for all!"

Shedding Old Skin

EPHESIANS 4:17-32

Living in a more country setting than ever before, I'm always intrigued about what I may find in my yard. One morning, I woke to let the dog out and saw a huge bull having breakfast in my front yard. The more interesting discoveries have been a deer hoof, which my dog decided to bring into the house, an entire rib skeleton of a deer, and feathers from a bird that didn't escape. Near my wild blackberry bushes, it's not abnormal to find a shed snakeskin. The fact that a snake got that close to me doesn't bring about a spirit of enthusiasm, but the remnant of its skin is better than the live deal.

Several creatures in this world shed their old skin or form to allow a new skin or form. For example, snakes, lizards, and amphibians routinely shed their skin. Even humans, in a way, shed old skin. So, the joke goes that the dust on one's bookshelf could be the shed skin of a loved one, which is why, the joke continues, that one doesn't wish to dust. They don't want to get rid of someone they know and love.

While skin shedding commonly occurs, getting rid of other old items in one's life is a different matter. Now, I'm not as bad as the hoarders featured on television shows, but I find it hard to get rid of old items. For example, in high school, I had a comfortable pair of old Converse tennis shoes. Unfortunately, the fabric had worn out right next to the plastic toe covering so that anyone could see what color of socks I was wearing. However, the shoes were so comfortable; I didn't want to work in a new pair.

I practice the same actions with automobiles. When I purchase a new or used car, I drive it until it dies or repairs start to cost the same as a monthly payment on another car. The first two cars titled in my name were a 1971 Gremlin and a 1979 Chevette. The Gremlin got me through college, the first few years of marriage, and the first semester of seminary. I was fortunate to work at my church's activities building during my last three years of college. A man who was in one of our bowling leagues, Bob Forrester, was accommodating in performing low-cost auto repairs for me. He viewed this service to me as a ministry to the Lord. That Gremlin did its best to confirm his calling over and over again.

While in Seminary in Fort Worth, I started work at the Polytechnic Baptist Church. As fortune would have it, there was an auto mechanic in the church. He began his work with the Gremlin as well. Finally, the Gremlin had seen its better days with its life on this earth. The mechanic jokingly said it would be best to drive the vehicle into Lake Arlington and collect on the insurance.

The Gremlin's ultimate demise led me to purchase the 1979 Chevette. The purchase occurred during the gas shortage in the late 1970s, so I went after a compact car with a standard transmission. The "Vette," as I called it, survived my first church due to the ministry of Barry Stefflen. God has been good to me in providing men with a calling to my auto repair. Barry tightened the clutch numerous times, put new brakes in, and repaired a leaky radiator.

The Vette made the journey with me to Natchez when I began serving a new church. But, unfortunately, its life was short-lived after that point, and once the Vette was beyond repair, another new automobile entered my life.

I don't like to part with old things.

At this chapter's writing, the University of Mississippi put a new carpet in my office and repainted the walls. I joked with the painters about the pastor's story, who kept adding turpentine to his paint to make it last longer. Finally, when he realized the paint job was terrible, he proclaimed he would "repaint, and thin no more."

The painters just stared at me blankly.

As I was boxing up my office for the renovations, I realized I had a lot of junk accumulate over fifteen years. So, I invited one of my students going into a camping ministry after graduation to come and take whatever books in camping and outdoor recreation I had. The book giveaway was a big step for me. I think you know by now that I'm not particularly eager to get rid of old things.

I wish this departing of old things only dealt with things. But, unfortunately, I also find it challenging to give up old habits, thoughts, and sins. Paul knew he dealt with this as well as his Ephesian friends; therefore, he addressed it in his cell call.

Paul reminds his Ephesian friends of how they used to be—living in confusion and darkness, with no sense of shame. They used to give in to any lustful pleasure and impurity. As I read Paul's cell call, I have to remember that although he was writing it to first-century friends, he could easily be writing the letter to me.

A skeptic might point out that the Ephesians Paul was talking to had already become Christians, so why are they being reminded about how they used to live? I can answer that out of my own life. My faith in Christ doesn't instantly cure me from temptation. In the book *Ragamuffin Gospel*, Brennan Manning, speaking on this very topic, points out:

> Often I have been asked, "Brennan, how is it possible that you became an alcoholic after you got saved?" It is possible because I got battered and bruised by loneliness and failure, because I got discouraged, uncertain, guilt-ridden, and took my eyes off Jesus. Because the Christ-encounter did not transfigure me into an angel. Because justification by grace through faith means I have been set in right relationship with God, not made the equivalent of a patient etherized on a table.[17]

---

[17] Brennan Manning, *The Ragamuffin Gospel* (Multnomah Publishing, 2000).

The most significant failures in my life occurred after I decided to follow and pattern my life after Jesus. Those sins before following Jesus included disobedience to parents, desires to hurt other children, and stealing that candy bar from the corner store on Twenty-Third Avenue in Independence, Missouri. However, after accepting Christ as my Savior, troubles caused me to take similar paths as Brennan Manning.

Paul continues his encouragement by reminding his friends and us to let our new nature take precedence over our old nature. Then, as if he were speaking to a future me, Paul gives a list of sins to stop doing. Verse 25, "Stop telling lies." OK, guilty as charged. Sometimes I like to embellish a story to make it funnier than the truth. If I don't confess to the embellishment, then I am lying. Point taken. Thanks, Paul.

He continues with more sins. Don't let anger control you, and especially don't let the sun go down while you're still angry. This approach will change my going to bed routine. Anger is dangerous, as it gives the devil a foothold on us. However, I found that a time-out from the rage and the disagreement so that a good night's sleep can occur is better than arguing until the wee hours of the morning with an alarm set for 5:00 a.m. After a restful night, both parties might realize the silliness of the argument. If not, at least both parties are well rested for a daylong bout.

"Stop stealing, use your hands for good hard work, and give generously to others in need" (verse 28). My thoughts take me back to the corner store candy copping caper, and I wonder if I can ever get past it. My heart reminds me that I don't always give my best in every situation, which is the same as stealing.

"Don't use foul or abusive language" (verse 29). I suddenly think of the popular social media meme that says, "I love Jesus, but I cuss a little." Paul points out a better use of our voice is in praising rather than profaning. Sometimes my tongue refuses to shed its old skin, and something foul or abusive pops out in certain situations. While I didn't curse a lot around my sons, they told me that when a swear word did pop out, they knew their behavior had crossed the line with me.

A CELL CALL FROM PAUL

Finally, Paul says to be kind, loving, and forgiving of one another, which is the best sign the old skin is gone and the new creation has taken over. So, perhaps I'll do another spring cleaning and get rid of stuff I'm not using anymore or shouldn't use. Sometimes, I've realized, I don't have room for the good or great news until I get rid of the useless or needless old.

We have a new nature and a new life in Christ. Let's enjoy it!

Dead Skunk Memories

Ephesians 5:1–20

Some people question why the chicken crossed the road, but I've never met a person who didn't wish that the skunk made it across without harm. Anyone who has passed the dead skunk scene immediately remembers the burning odor that seems to stay in the nostrils forever.

I recently went to the grocery store when I encountered not one but two dead skunks within a mile of each other on a county road near my house. As funny as it seems, the foul odor started a chain reaction in my memory banks. My initial thoughts regarding the "air out there" was how a reference to the aroma could be a good way of poking fun at my brothers and the years of growing up sharing various fragrances.

My younger brother Mark and I shared a bedroom from his arrival in this world until a few months before my wedding. We were notorious for sharing particular things. Dirty socks and underwear in pillowcases were among the fare we shared. It was not rare for us to go from one end of the house to the other to share some aroma. We were the perfect balance between brotherly love and sibling rivalry.

The thoughts of my brothers then extended to the friends my younger brother and I hung out with in college. We had a similar orientation to foul smells. So, we created a rating system to determine the odor's strength by the size of a room or building where the scent would cause an evacuation. So, when one of us experienced a foul odor, they would exclaim, "That would empty a phone booth, large classroom, football stadium, and so on."

The thought process went from those friends to some others in high school. One of the group projects conducted in junior English class was the portrayal of some advertisements. My group chose to perform a used-car commercial. My nickname in high school was Pierre, so we added the only French name we could think of, which happened to be a famous skunk that appeared in the *Looney Tunes* cartoons named Pepe Le Pew. So, the used-car salesman was named Pierre Pepe Le Pew.

I then thought about a statement made by my first daughter-in-law about the differences between little girls and little boys. Jerilyn and my oldest son, James, gave me my first granddaughter, and later they awarded me my first grandson. During a visit a couple of years after Jed's birth, Jerilyn told me one of the differences between raising a daughter and a son was in the son's delight and pride in making certain aromas. I let her know that boys never really outgrow that sense of pride.

All of those thoughts came from an encounter with two dead skunks. Foul aromas are prevalent enough that deodorizing sprays and perfumes are billion-dollar industries. People will do anything to get rid of the bad smell.

The triggering of memories is quite a unique subject. A few years ago, one of our graduate assistants conducted extensive research about memory, even appearing for a Ted Talk regarding the issue. The more enjoyable odorous memories I have deal with more enjoyable memories. For example, whenever I smell fresh bread baking, I think of my maternal grandmother. She could bake bread as one can only dream of, such as yeast rolls and homemade bread smothered with butter and honey. Anytime I pass a sandwich shop that bakes bread, my mom's mom comes to my mind.

When I smell wood burning, it reminds me of camping adventures around a campfire. I also think of another love of mine in barbecuing. Smelling wood burning makes me think about some of the most delicious ribs, chicken, pulled pork, brisket, and steak I've enjoyed over the years. It's as if the aroma of the smoke automatically triggers the taste in my memory.

When I open the door to a car and get that new car smell, my memory takes me back to the first new car I ever purchased. During my first year of seminary, I drove my college car, a 1971 Gremlin. When it needed a fourth round of repairs in Fort Worth, a mechanic from the church where I worked recommended driving the car into Lake Arlington and getting the insurance rather than fixing it one more time. The car trouble occurred during the gas shortage of 1979, so my wife at the time and I went shopping for a standard-shift automobile. The main difficulty was that neither of us knew how to drive a stick shift at the time. I still laugh at the salesman's patience as I practiced the "grind 'em 'til you find 'em" method of shifting gears. I'm grateful I didn't scare any other kind of aroma out of the salesman during the test drive.

While reading this, you have probably had memories of some good and bad odors from your life. One of the most pleasant aromas I've read about is the one mentioned in Ephesians, chapter 5. Paul offers this advice to the followers of Jesus in his cell call to Ephesus: "Live a life filled with love, following the example of Christ. He loved us and offered himself as a sacrifice for us, a pleasing aroma to God" (Ephesians 5:1–2 NLT).

When preparing for a date or an appointment, I make sure I'm cleaned up and smelling good. The aroma can create either a positive or negative atmosphere around you. Paul says if we live like the example of Jesus in loving others, the aroma gets to heaven, and God enjoys it. However, to benefit the Ephesians, Paul went through many sins that don't smell good at all. Having been found guilty of the entire list, I know that these sins can stink up relationships, employment situations, and the trust of others.

Paul further warns the believers not to be fooled by people who excuse these sins and live disobediently toward God. "For you were once full of darkness," Paul says, "but now you have light from the Lord. So, live as people of light" (Ephesians 5:8 NLT). By the shining of this light in our lives, we will discover places that are still stinky.

Paul advises, "be filled with the Holy Spirit, singing psalms and hymns and spiritual songs among yourselves, and making music to the Lord in your hearts" (Ephesians 5:18a–19). Our proper worship will assist us in living by the Spirit's power and going back to creating that sweet aroma God loves to smell.

While we are on the topic of aromas, Paul closes out this section of his letter reminding the Ephesians that it is better to be filled with the Spirit than to be drunk with wine. Our department at Ole Miss used to conduct a Halloween event called the Haunted Trail. We sponsored it along with the Oxford Park Commission. Our students would serve as tour guides through the trail and set up different scary scenes. It was quite the change for me after a twenty-year career in church recreation, where we avoided the frightening activities around Halloween alternative carnivals.

One year, a representative from the Park Commission informed me that he smelled alcohol around some students. The aroma of intoxication, as well as the behavior of the intoxicated, is quite apparent. As a result, we excused the student from service for the rest of the evening. In addition, he also faced other consequences of a foolish choice.

Paul refers to the choice between the two as being wise or foolish. Paul says it's better for those following Jesus to fill themselves with the Holy Spirit. Ironically, when the first group of believers experienced the power of the Holy Spirit, the crowd accused them of being drunk (Acts 2:13). I take this to mean that Paul was advising the Ephesians to have a celebratory attitude and action by giving control of their lives to the Spirit rather than wine. Being filled with the Spirit leads to "singing psalms and hymns and spiritual songs among yourselves, and making music to the Lord in your heart" (Ephesians 5:19 NLT). These verses and advice are not a warning against any alcohol use but rather a warning about the overuse of alcohol. So, let's not mistake the meaning here.

So, let's forget the deodorant sprays and other perfumed cover-ups. Instead, let's live a life full of the Spirit, and we will all make a pleasing aroma for God and those around us.

Wait! What's in It for Me?

Ephesians 5:21–6:4

The phrase "what's in it for me" drives a lot of my actions and behaviors. For example, if I attended such a meeting as Selfish People Anonymous, I would introduce myself, "Hi, my name is Dave, and I'm a selfish person."

When I teach university classes for upcoming sports and recreation leaders, I inform them that all they do in this industry is customer related. In other words, stress the benefits of participation or answer their question, "What's in it for me?" If the answer to that question is positive for a person, then a sale or participation in an activity or event occurs. This particular question drives our purchases, volunteer opportunities, and, I'm sad to say, our relationships.

In just about every relationship I've ever had, I seek what's in it for me. I've been on both sides of the give-and-take relationships where one person does all the giving, and the other does all the taking. These relationships usually end when one of us gets smart as to what is happening.

In this portion of Paul's cell call to the Ephesians, he lays out some heavy relationship advice—that being, submit to one another. Therein lies my problem. I'm not really good at submission.

When I was growing up, I used to think my father had the best hearing ever. He could tell me to do something, and I would mutter a rebellious and nonsubmissive statement under my breath, and somehow he heard it and would ask me again what I said. But, of course, my response was always "Nothing."

I used the same behavior against teachers and supervisors as well. I have discovered that I am gifted with excellent passive-aggressive attributes. This behavior is because I'm not particularly eager to submit to authority. However, I've learned caution in saying things to myself rather than under my breath or out loud.

I was in a ministerial staff meeting at one of the churches I worked with when the pastor reminded the entire staff to be more active with one of the events in the church that demanded total ministerial attendance. I looked around the table and saw a few of us present at this particular activity every week. I saw some who attended occasionally and a couple who were rarely, if ever, in attendance. The reminder struck my antisubmission attitude, which led me to say, "Which ones of us in particular need to be more active, Pastor?"

The pastor replied, "All of us do."

I didn't let the point die. After all, the aggressive part of me was rolling by now. So, I pushed it a couple more times until the pastor aggressively said one last time, "Waddell, all of us do!"

This selfish lack of a submissive attitude makes me the worst possible source to discuss the family of which Paul wrote in this cell call to the Ephesians. When I discuss marriage issues with people, I jokingly tell them to "always ask the divorced guy for advice."

A friend of mine was having some difficulties in her marriage. At one point, I encountered her sitting alone at a bar, where I approached her to see how things were going in her relationship. She told me the marriage didn't have much of a chance. I asked if they would consider counseling, and she said, "Probably not."

I pointed to my face and drew a circle around it with my finger. Then I said, "Just know, this is the best that's out there for women over fifty in this town."

She looked off and said, "Well, maybe we can try counseling."

I'm happy to announce they are still married to this day.

While I teach at the University of Mississippi, my ordination in the ministry is still active. Therefore, I have officiated several weddings for former students. I've performed more weddings as a college instructor than I ever did as a minister on staff in a church.

During one of those ceremonies, I had some time to kill between a Friday evening rehearsal and the late Saturday-afternoon wedding. So, I found a seafood restaurant where I conversed with a lady sitting by herself. We talked long enough to share a few life stories. After hearing mine, she asked, "If you're divorced, why are you helping other people get married?"

The truth is I still believe in the value of marriage even though I fouled up my own. Paul's cell call to assist his married Ephesian friends also helps me realize the error of my ways in marriage. Submitting to one another is the best version of the give-and-take approach to a relationship.

When I was approaching my marriage, Gerald, the music minister at our church, commented on the fifty-fifty approach to marriage, where everything was equal in the give and take. However, he had a different mathematical formula. He said the procedure should go "sixty-forty both ways." In other words, perfect submission in a give-and-take relationship would demonstrate each person trying to outgive the other without concern about the score ever being even. Fifty-fifty will always have us looking for more of "What's in it for me?"

Paul wanted to remind his Ephesian friends how the married life demonstrates God's love for all people. The picture a marriage portrays is the same as the relationship Jesus has with His church. Jesus, through His love, gave His life for the church. Likewise, the husband is to submit his life to his wife. In the same way the church serves Jesus, the wife submits her service to her husband. Thus, the "what's in it for me" is defined by how well one serves, loves, and respects the other. By the way, the math of marriage Paul describes would indicate an equal sign, =, and not a greater than, >, or lesser than, <, sign.

Paul points out the mystery of a man leaving his family and uniting with his wife to become one. I use this principle when I teach first aid to demonstrate how to apply a bandage. First, one wraps the bandage around the wound. Then a portion of the bandage is pulled out and doubled up. Then the doubled-up part ties a knot with the remaining part of the bandage. So, I explain, "The two become one (doubled-up bandage part becoming one piece), and it joins another to tie the knot."

Paul concludes this section with the aspect of parenthood. The whole idea of parenthood brings about an entirely different version of submission and "what's in it for me." Once that little one pops out of the womb, life changes. My weekly golf outings disappeared altogether. Spontaneous trips become planned vacations. Suitcases multiply for a journey with several changes of clothes and boxes of diapers. The addition of children affects decisions one might make in careers, finances, home ownership, and more. Parents have to submit to the needs of their children in every aspect of life. Jesus did this Himself when He left the glory of heaven to join us on earth to cover the debt of our sins. The "what's in it for me" occurs when you see your children grown, gone, great, and possibly giving you grandchildren.

Later in life, I had the opportunity to go back home and serve alongside Gerald. He is the father of three sons, just as I am. I attempted connecting with each son in something they enjoyed. With my oldest, it was our Driveway Basketball League. With the middle son, it was video games, movies, and theater. The youngest seemed to enjoy debates and argumentation. As my boys grew older, it became very apparent that they were winning more battles than losing. I asked Gerald how I should deal with how my sons were becoming better than me in many facets of life. He gave me great advice when he said, "You start teaching them how to be a gracious loser." The "what's in it for me" is in watching my sons father their children. They make me proud.

Finally, Paul warns fathers not to treat children in such a way as to provoke them into anger. Being such a teaser and joker, I may have pushed the limit on this guidance. I love the New International Version that says, "Fathers, do not exasperate your children" (Ephesians 6:4 NIV). I suppose I did all right, as each of my sons became great men. I tell people that one of my desires of fatherhood was that each son would be better and more accomplished than I am. Each one had met this goal by the time they were twelve years old. They've only gotten better since that time.

So, how's your submission in relationships looking? Need a little more sixty-forty in your life? Paul wrote this encouragement, knowing his friends would start improving their submission at that point. Want to join in with us? You'll discover more of "what's in it for me" than you could have ever imagined!

Employee Handbook

Ephesians 6:5-9

I cannot imagine what life would be like if I were to be a slave. I tease about how I felt like a slave while growing up, but it's pretty easy to see how privileged I was in those years. I see series like *Roots* or movies like *Twelve Years a Slave* and get a glimpse of what it may have been like, but unless I lived through it, I could not come close to imagining the daily struggle of being someone's property.

Following Paul's advice on marriage and parenthood, he submitted a short word to the slaves of Ephesus. He wanted to advise on how to be a follower of Christ and a slave at the same time. From his letter to Philemon, I surmise that Paul didn't support keeping Christians under the bondage of human slavery. In other letters, Paul refers to being a slave for Christ, placing our lives entirely under Jesus's direction. That particular analogy would also make a difference in catching the modern message from this first-century letter.

So, how am I to get a modern message from Paul's first-century cell call? I choose to read the verses in the context of employer and employee. While an employment situation is nowhere close to the ravages of slavery, I can glean some truth about my situation in life. So, for this chapter, I will compare the master with the employer and the slave with the employee.

Paul starts by imploring his slave friends to serve with deep respect and fear. Thanks, Paul. That's strike one for me. Far too often in my career, I've let circumstances and employer decisions remove my respect for my supervisors. I've been guilty of talking about them behind their back. I've done it enough that I have often encouraged those I lead the freedom to whine or complain about me behind my back because I know people tend to do so. However, when I lost respect for the person, I honestly tried to respect their position. I may have disagreed with their decision or direction, but I recognized their position to make such a call.

A few years ago, my department chair decided to use an available position in the recreation area and transform it into an exercise science faculty slot. Our department housed both programs. I went to him and shared my thoughts and feelings as to why it was a wrong decision. Mark thanked me at the end of the conversation and declared he would stick with his original decision. At that point, I said, without using sarcasm, "I like this plan! What can I do to help?"

I realized I needed to respect his leadership despite the disagreement.

Next, Paul tells his friends and us to please our employers all the time and not just when they are watching us. I had the privilege for seven years of doing some summer consulting with the Kirby Pines Estates in Memphis, Tennessee. I worked there once as the activities director. When I began my work at the University of Mississippi, Annette Marlar, the director of medical services, would hire me to work a few weeks out of the summer when I didn't have class responsibilities to assist with various projects. The managing company for Kirby Pines was the Retirement Communities of America, led by Charlie Trammell.

A few of those years, I had the opportunity to give an educational presentation during their staff retreat. One of the retreat topics dealt with gaining a greater performance out of the entire staff. When Mr. Trammell was present, I noticed that the staff made sure to do their work quickly and efficiently. However, I also noticed when Charlie was not present; the staff didn't work as hard. Somehow the staff created a communication pipeline to let everyone know when Charlie entered the premises. Knowing this, I created the acronym WHICH for What Happens If Charlie's Here. The phrase encouraged the staff to work as hard as they would if Charlie was in the facility.

I think Paul would have liked my acronym.

Paul gives the following encouragement to work with enthusiasm and act as though you are working for God instead of your employer. One of the aspects of leadership I attempt to teach to my students is how contagious enthusiasm can be. I'd be silly to recommend a high level of enthusiasm every day on the job. I doubt that is humanly possible. I tell the students, for those unenthusiastic days, to fake it 'til they make it. I challenge them to find the days I may not come to class with full enthusiasm. There are relationships where I can be honest about my days where I lack enthusiasm, but it's not to my employer or my students.

Finally, Paul closes this part of his cell call with an encouraging word to the employers. Treat your employees without threats, and remember we are all working for the same Boss, who doesn't have any favorites.

I have been blessed over the years to have worked with great leaders. I mentioned some in the stories earlier in this chapter. Each of them taught me incredible lessons that helped shape who I am today. My first boss of note was Bobby Shows, who helped form my calling into ministry. Wilton Anthony, or, as we called him, Brother Tony, led my first full-time church. Brother Tony is in his mideighties and still pastoring full-time. In Natchez, Mississippi, Brother Puckett was the first senior pastor who had me preach in the church. Although, I did ask him to stop announcing my preaching so that more people would accidentally be in attendance. It was challenging preaching only to family, a few friends, and the people who weren't present Sunday morning to hear the announcement.

Mark Loftin and I worked together for seven years before a promotion took him to the dean's office. Mark picked up on how to deal with me beautifully. For example, he asked me how the time off had gone for me after one Christmas break. I told him that it was a wonderful time, as I got paid during the time off but not doing anything for work. He jokingly asked what was different in that from the regular semester. Another time, I lamented that I wished my salary could equal what I felt I was worth. Hearing this, Mark teasingly reminded me that Mississippi had a minimum wage law.

It's not easy leading people, which is why Paul pointed out for masters or, in this case, supervisors to treat their slaves or employees in a way that glorifies Christ.

Getting Ready to Get Ready

EPHESIANS 6:10–24

At Ole Miss, every athletic event begins with someone screaming, "Are you ready!" At that point, the fans scream the famous Hotty Toddy chant. It is tempting to start my classes that way. I don't mean to brag, but I have made getting ready an art form! I am a firm believer in being organized. Early in my church work career, I felt a lack of organization and took a course in time management. I purchased a couple of books to organize my work better and ensure I was getting done what was supposed to get done. I knew preparation was a crucial component in doing any job well.

The course and books were beneficial. I learned how I should prioritize my task list and keep an organized calendar. I purchased a Day-Timer package, including a pocket-sized notebook to effortlessly keep the task list and calendar dates. I carried the little notebook with me to work and church to keep track of any commitments I made along the way. I prioritized the task list as A, B, or C, depending on its importance. I further classified the list by marking the items as A-1, A-2, B-1, and so on. The idea of prioritization was to get the essential things done first.

The calendar pages had a monthly calendar to view, and the layout of each day's schedule appeared in half-hour time slots. Of course, the idea here is to write in essential appointments to keep the said appointments. After starting this process, I learned a crucial lesson: I have to *look* at the list and the calendar after listing an item.

One Sunday morning, one of the ladies in the church asked

if I could come to the school library and tell stories the following month. She was the school librarian and reasoned I might be an entertaining guest. I was all too delighted to do so and immediately wrote the appointment into the appropriate time slot. Unfortunately, I went to work that day and began the everyday work I had to do. I received a phone call that morning from the librarian. She started the conversation by asking how I was doing. I responded positively, to which she asked, "Is there somewhere you're supposed to be today?"

I responded that I didn't think so as I grabbed my pocket calendar. There was silence on the phone as the librarian allowed me to get myself into trouble. The calendar indicated that I had the appointment and that I was already ten minutes late. She was kind enough to rearrange the appointment for another day. I made several reminders so that I wouldn't miss the rescheduled date.

"Are you ready?" Being prepared is a crucial component of doing any job well.

I held various jobs between working in a church and my work at the University of Mississippi, one of which was a company that conducted leadership training for businesses. I studied and became a big fan of leadership during my last few years at Germantown Baptist Church, so I thought it would be a good fit for me. I'm not sure if the employer didn't tell me, or I just heard what I wanted to hear, but the leadership training only occurred if I could recruit business leaders into the course. To recruit, I was in a position of cold-calling business professionals, contacting them with no reference in the Memphis area, and setting an appointment to meet with them.

From the few that occurred, the meetings consisted of me telling them why they were terrible at leadership and how, for $4,000, I could make them better. Each morning, I would arrive at the office and prepare for the day. First, I'd line out the businesses I would target that day and put the list directly next to the phone. Then I would get a cup of coffee and take a couple of sips. Next, I would look over the list and highlight the ones I thought would be the best bet to set an appointment with me. Then I would numerically order those highlighted potential clients. An hour would go by before I even picked up the phone. My supervisor said I was the best he'd ever seen at getting ready to get ready. I smiled, but I don't think he meant it as a compliment.

"Are you ready?" Being prepared is a crucial component of doing any job well.

In the three months of work with that company, I faced rejection or postponement more than I ever remember. I was, however, able to set up four appointments, of which two agreed to purchase the program. Regrettably, the owner of the company met with those two for the leadership consultation rather than me. It's a shame the owner met with those two because I could have done well getting ready to get ready for the training.

"Are you ready?" Being prepared is a crucial component of doing any job well.

In his cell call to the church in Ephesus, Paul knew of this very preparation issue, explaining the preparations that followers of Jesus must take when going out into the world. Paul warned that if we are not fully prepared, we stand no chance against the schemes of the devil. Paul compared our readiness to a soldier getting dressed.

First of all, Paul said to put on a belt of truth. I understand this reference best when going through security at an airport and placing the belt in the tray. When the TSA agent tells me to hold my arms above my head, I try to expand my stomach. I pray the pants don't fall at that time. Belts are great at holding things up and being flexible to meet the needs of the wearer. If I lose an inch, the belt adjusts for the loss. If I happen to gain an inch, the belt goes another notch to help me. The belt Paul tells us to wear helps hold the body armor of God's righteousness. In other words, the belt helps us hold up that which is most beneficial.

The belt holds the body armor of God's righteousness and serves the purpose of protecting the soldier's most vital organs. There have been times in life when I met a particular lady who created a desire in me to know her more, and friends told me to guard my heart. Paul knew the devil wants nothing more than to put a fiery arrow smack into our hearts. Preparing ourselves with God's body armor of righteousness protects the very organs that keep us connected to God.

Years ago, the Nike shoe company featured advertisements attributing the amazing talents of the basketball player Michael Jordan to the Nike shoes he wore. The commercial would demonstrate impressive basketball moves by Jordan and then give the phrase, "It's gotta be the shoes."[18] In Paul's case here, it is definitely "the shoes!"

The shoes, which represent the readiness to preach the Good News of peace with God, come with cleats so that we may stand firm and not slide around. We also know that the feet tire quickly without good shoes, and with tired feet, we are not suitable for anything but sitting on the sideline.

Paul also said we should carry a shield of faith. Of course, I can't talk about shields without referring to the comic book hero Captain America, who used the shield as a defense against attack and a weapon against his enemies. The shield Paul uses as a metaphor stands as tall as the soldier. It would be covered in leather so that a fiery arrow would hit the shield, and the leather would put out the flame. It is our faith that keeps the devil from destroying us.

Paul knew the helmet was also a crucial bit of dress for the soldier. He refers to it as the helmet of salvation. Helmets are well-known in our culture. Most states or communities require the wearing of a protective helmet when riding a bicycle or motorcycle. A famous comedian had a routine where he wondered about the effectiveness of helmets worn by skydiving people. He has a good point. The helmet Paul speaks of had padding on the inside so that the soldier could wear the protective piece comfortably. The helmet consisted of hard metal on the outside, so arrows and spears would deflect without harm. This helmet of salvation serves the same purpose, deflecting ugly or wrong thoughts from getting inside our heads.

Finally, Paul gets to the primary weapon for a soldier, that being a sword. The sword of the Spirit is the Word of God. I remember as a child participating in what was called a Bible drill. We memorized

---

[18] https://www.youtube.com/watch?v=fkY7W6kCRY4.

scriptures and learned to find the reference in the Bible in as little time as possible in a contest. First, the children would line up with their Bibles at their side. Then the leader would prompt us by saying, "Draw swords." At this point, we held our Bibles in front of us, ready to hear the verse called out and to find the scripture hurriedly.

In recent years, the "draw swords" command has become "present Bibles." I suppose I shall "saber" the memory of drawing swords during my Bible drill days. From Christ's example, Paul knew that we are useless in a battle with the devil unless we go into the fight with God's Word. When Satan tempted Jesus, His reply was always to quote scripture. I have found scripture defeats evil thoughts much better than my sense of logic in my own life.

So, how are you doing? Are you ready?

PAUL'S LETTER TO THE
PHILIPPIANS

The city of Philippi was a strategic trade location, on the east-west Egnation Highway between Rome and Asia. While the Romans desired the city to be a miniature version of Rome, they never erased their Greek-Hellenistic culture. The city had many gods worshiped there; however, a limited Jewish population meant there was no synagogue in the community. The lack of a synagogue reflects the requirement to have at least ten married Jewish men establish a synagogue in a community.[19]

The city received its name from Philip I of Macedon, the father of Alexander the Great. Augustus became a Roman colony following the Battle of Philippi, where Antony and Octavius killed Brutus and Cassius in 42 BC.[20]

Paul knew the community well as he started the church there, following an earthshaking experience. When imprisoned in town for preaching the Gospel, an earthquake shook the prison bars away, and the prison guard responsible for Paul and others started believing in Jesus.

Paul's letter came when the church needed a word of encouragement due to some preacher jealousy and the Judaisers pushing the idea that one must first become a Jew before becoming a Christian.[21]

---

[19] Thompsons, p. 1539.
[20] https://www.biblestudytools.com/blogs/matthew-s-harmon/the-city-of-philippi-in-the-bible.html.
[21] https://www.padfield.com/acrobat/history/philippi.pdf.

A Silent Minute for Those Closest to Me

PHILIPPIANS 1:3–11

I can't watch *It's a Beautiful Day in the Neighborhood* or *Won't You Be My Neighbor* without getting emotional whenever the movie refers to Mr. Roger's gift of a silent minute. Fred Rogers explained it during his commencement address to the graduates of Dartmouth College.

> I'd like to give you all an invisible gift. A gift of a silent minute to think about those who have helped you become who you are today.
>
> So, let's just take a minute, in honor of those that have cared about us all along the way. One silent minute ...[22], [23]

Before writing this section of the cell call, Paul may have had a silent minute to remember his Philippian friends. He talks about how he gives thanks to God every time he thinks about them. Paul was appreciative of how these friends helped spread the Good News about Jesus. He also believes they will stay true to the task of becoming

---

[22] https://www.saltproject.org/progressive-christian-blog/fred-rogers-one-minute-of-silence.

[23] One can view the entire speech at https://www.youtube.com/watch?v=907yEkALaAY.

more Christlike from that point until the day of Christ's return to this earth.

I will take a minute break as I write this to consider the people who make my list.

Please allow me to share mine, as several people pop into my mind. I always begin with my family. First is my father, who taught me so much about life. He encouraged my athletic dreams, despite recognizing I had such little talent to succeed. He exhibited ethical behavior. He always seemed present for me. Even during the tumultuous teenage years, I felt like I could talk to him if needed. In 2002, he left us to go fishing with Simon Peter, James, and John in heaven. When I speak, I sense he is still with us because I've become more and more like him. Likewise, thoughts of my mother arise as well. Her advice and prayers have shaped me significantly. She taught me how to accept gifts graciously, among many other lessons. Finally, my older and younger brothers are prototypical male siblings. They can pick on me, but we have a battle on our hands if anyone else does so.

The names Bobby Shows and Wayne Dismuke pop up. These two men were the activities director and youth minister during my high school and college years in Springfield, Missouri. Bobby saw something in me and used me in church camps and social events. His leadership led me to pursue a career in recreation, where I have served for all but fourteen months since 1975. Wayne was one of the first church leaders who appreciated my sense of humor and directed me to minister through humor. Both of these men recently departed to heaven as well. I hope they're not telling my dad about some things I did that he may have never known about me.

Wilton Anthony, or as we called him, Brother Tony, was the first pastor I worked with on a church staff. He demonstrated that one could have fun while working in the church. If I were to comment on all the pranks and fun we had, the book would be the size of *War and Peace*.

Odean Puckett, affectionately known as Brother Puckett, was another pastor who greatly influenced me. He was soft-spoken and reserved; however, he also knew how to pack a humorous punch. I went into one staff meeting with the Ed McMahon Ten Million Dollar sweepstakes that came out annually. The envelope always read, "You may be the winner of Ten Million Dollars!" I placed my copy in front of him before one staff meeting and told him, "The money problems in our church are solved. It looks like I'm the winner!"

Brother Puckett leaned back in his chair and asked, "David, what would you do with that money if you won it?"

I declared, "I'd give half of it to the church."

Brother Puckett quickly quipped, "Then I know why you haven't won it yet. God knows how you'd spend the other half."

The sad part is he's correct. Brother Puckett allowed me to preach and pushed the level of biblical knowledge and understanding in my life. I still have a Bible full of sermon notes from my years under his leadership.

Then there's Lewis DeCarlo, mentioned in an earlier chapter. Lewis was one of our baseball coaches at Germantown Baptist Church. Later, he opened a café and bookstore in the church. He was available to do so because he ethically rejected an offer at work that was not legal, which led to his termination. Lewis has stuck with me through the highs and lows of life and never considered throwing me away. Here's how amazing God works: Lewis is a New York Yankee and Auburn Tiger fan, two of the teams my teams always hate to lose to in sports.

There's a collection of men I attended seminary with or knew from my days in church recreation: John Longworth, Chuck Williamson, Jo Batson, Dean Finch, Greg Windham, Charlie Reavis, Dale Adkins, Bob Farmer, and Dale Connally. After I resigned from church work due to revealed sin in my life, these men never let our relationship die and were constant encouragers toward my healing and restoration. It's a thrill to still be connected so closely to these gentlemen.

Kim Spillers, Cathy Moss, Brittany Applewhite, Cindy Hogan, Bill Grady, Becky Peters, Leigh Ann Teague, and other Facebook friends were some of the first people to encourage me to pursue writing. Kim commented on many of my Facebook posts when I began to write more and requested my *Top Ten Reasons I Was Glad I Had Atrial Fibrillation* to be put into book form and presented to her for her birthday. I found a binding company to place it in hardcover, and to this day, she's the only one who owns all of my books in hardcover copies. Cindy encouraged me to write by telling me my stories would have meaning to people who didn't already know me. So, if you don't like my writing, you can blame these people.

I worked with Annette Marlar in two separate sections of my life, the first as an employee of Kirby Pines Estates, and later as a consultant for the same company. Unaware that I was in one of my down moments in life, she commented that I had no idea how influential I was to this world. Her comment made me create a silent minute where I could also consider the number of people God allowed me to impact and influence. In the leadership class I instruct for sport and recreation students, I have them consider both someone who impacted them and someone they've influenced in life. Remembering the influence you've shared in life could be a fascinating silent minute as well. I like to repeat both silent minutes to remember all the people like Paul did with his Philippian friends.

I must also add my three sons. I admire how mature and wise they are. They must have gotten it from their mother. It's like a comical and joyful slap in the face when they demonstrate greater faith, wisdom, and forgiveness than I do in a particular moment or situation. They often remind me Jesus died for those who have offended them. In those moments, I'm more like James and John when they asked Jesus if He wanted them to pray down fire from heaven to consume some ugly Samaritans. I'm glad my sons know better.

So many others pop into my mind, as they have played a role at different moments in my life. Forgive me for not listing all of those names. I've discovered that sometimes I need more than one minute to consider all the people who have impacted me the way the Philippians influenced Paul. Perhaps it would have been easier in this chapter had I lumped them all together, as Paul did. This way, you get to enjoy my silent minute or minutes as well.

Paul speaks of how he prays for his Philippian friends and how joyful he feels having partnered with them to share the Gospel of Jesus with others. Paul mentions how special they are in that, while he is in prison, they fill his thoughts and prayers. Paul prays for them to let their love overflow and to keep growing in their knowledge and understanding. With Paul's free time in a prison cell, I imagine that he spent numerous silent moments remembering how his friends had influenced him and how he influenced those same friends.

Paul concludes by admitting it's natural to feel about his friends the way he does. He states that God knows how much he loves these people. Paul mentions the special favor they offer as he is in prison and confirms the Good News of the Gospel. He wishes they would continue to grow in their righteous character and be filled with God's Spirit as they live pure and blameless lives.

I like how Paul may be the one thought of by so many Philippians and how many Philippians make Paul's silent minute. So, working off the idea I received after hearing Annette, let's take a minute to consider those who God has allowed us to impact and influence.

I imagine this minute will be just as rewarding.

A Different Kind of Prison

PHILIPPIANS 1:12–19

I was happy serving in my home church when the opportunity came to go to another church. Because of the leadership of my soon-to-be predecessor, this particular church had a reputation throughout the Southern Baptist Convention as being one of the most vital church recreation programs in the country. A couple of friends had submitted my name, so the church contacted me for my résumé and later conducted an interview. Everything must have gone well because they offered me the job, and I started in early September.

The usual conference I attended for church recreators happened every year in January in central Florida. I registered for the event, and a few weeks before we met, I got a call from one of the conference organizers. He wanted to warn me that some people in attendance at the conference might be upset with me. He pointed out that some felt they were more qualified for the job, yet somehow I ended up with it.

I thanked him for the warning but reminded him quickly that all of those people *were* more qualified than me. However, for some reason, God put me in the church instead of them. I understood how they felt. I had interviewed or submitted my name to various churches and never received a follow-up call. Some of the churches where I applied have not contacted me to this day. I feel sure a couple of those churches from the 1980s will call any day now.

I'd love to say there's no jealousy in ministry, but I can't. In seminary, I was jealous of those who worked in the seminary's recreation center. For the first twelve years of my ministry, I was jealous of those who didn't have youth ministry in their position title. I thoroughly enjoyed the teenagers I worked with, but I was still jealous of those with only the recreation responsibility in their title. For the next six years, I was jealous of those in larger churches. When I accepted a position in a larger church, I was jealous of those who got more stage time in worship services. After leaving church work, a group of accountability friends knew I was in trouble when I confessed I was jealous of a friend in prison because he didn't have to face the difficulties in life that I was going through. Jealousy is a trait that does not allow one to enjoy their current circumstances. Jealousy keeps us from contentment. Jealousy locks us up in its version of prison. In Monopoly terms, we don't get to pass go or collect $200. Jealousy puts us straight into jail until we draw a "Get out of Jail Free" card or roll doubles.

The jealousy continues in my life, despite me knowing better. My church in Oxford was fortunate one Sunday to enlist Tim Tebow to speak at both of our Sunday-morning services. Tebow was in town to cover the Ole Miss game for the SEC Television Network, making it easier for our church to book him. I was the children's ministry storyteller at the time, so I usually made it early, before the first service took place. As I approached the church, the parking lot was already full, and cars were parking illegally on a state highway. I found a spot in the funeral home parking lot across the street and walked into the church. I admit, to begin with, I'm skeptical of celebrity Christianity, and that attitude did not help me on this day.

The children's ministry leadership had to move the children to another location because the growing crowd of people to hear Mr. Tebow required the use of our room as an overflow room. I found where the children were hiding and discovered the revised schedule did not need my storytelling that morning. I waited in the hallway with friends, and my sarcastic skepticism kicked in. I asked our associate pastor, if I were to touch the hem of Tebow's blue jeans, would I be able to play college football? He knew me well enough to ignore me. My skepticism of celebrity Christianity grew as I watched people enter with excitement not typically seen in the churches I had served and attended. I wondered out loud if Jesus could have drawn the same crowd that Tebow was getting. Finally, frustrated with the circus atmosphere, I left and visited another previously attended church in Oxford.

The pastor at my former church announced his sermon title, "Saul's Jealousy of King David."

Ouch. I realized two things at that point. One, God has an incredible sense of humor and timing to set me up as He did. Second, my feelings of skepticism weren't about celebrity Christianity as much as it was that I was not a Christian celebrity. My jealousy was a prison sentence that kept me from worship, growth, and service that day.

Despite the jealousy throughout my life, good things happened for the Gospel during those years. Jealousy doesn't necessarily kill the outcome. Paul reminds the Philippians that one's motivation doesn't necessarily stop the truth from coming out. Let me explain more. During a rough period in my life, I obtained a copy of a book written by a famous television evangelist. The book was beneficial to me in healing from a significant setback in my life. This particular pastor has a large following in his community and worldwide, but he is also a target of all kinds of criticism. Some of the basis for the criticism is on doctrine. I often wonder if the jealousy of his success drives the criticism even more.

The church at Philippi must have had several preachers visiting and speaking. Some saw themselves as rivals of Paul for various reasons. I understand this from my previous years of wishing I was in someone else's place of service. Paul points out that despite the jealousy demonstrated by the "rivals," as long as there is preaching of the Gospel, it's all good. Paul avoided the dreaded comparison game. Paul realized he didn't have to win the Preacher of the Year award. Paul points out their motives may be selfish, and they may be doing it to make his prison stay a bit more troublesome. However, in the end, Jesus is preached, so it's a victory in Paul's mind. It's a win-win. Paul may have been behind bars, but the rivals were locked up worse than he was.

Paul then speaks of another win-win, which is whether it's best to go on to heaven or remain on earth. Paul saw both as having certain advantages. I contemplated this dilemma sitting in a hospital bed in 2012 with a heart condition called atrial fibrillation, or A-fib. Defined, A-fib is where half of a heart pumps blood normally, and the other half dances and quivers in place. I watched the Food Network on television for a while that first evening without knowing how bad of shape I was in with my heart. I realized watching people cook with butter, fat, and all kinds of meats might not be the best way to spend my time. I turned off the television and sat in my room alone and quiet. I was ready to go, should God decide I'd been around long enough. I also saw the advantage in sticking around. I wanted to see my grandchildren graduate and become adults. I wanted to make it long enough to be more than a good grandpa and see my grandkids have kids, thus making me a great-grandpa.

As you can tell, by the publication date of this book, God decided to leave me here for a little longer. Paul reminds me in his cell call to enjoy life on earth as if I were already a citizen of heaven. Avoid intimidation by those who are against you. Accept the suffering this life brings the same way Jesus accepted His suffering. I confess I'm still learning this lifestyle.

Paul accepts his role as a suffering prisoner. Despite being in prison, Paul demonstrates the freedom he has in Christ by living as an example for the rest of us the same way we should be examples for one another. While I was jealous of another prisoner earlier in life, I think I'd do better to live life out like the prisoner Paul did. Paul doesn't allow himself to live in a world of unfair comparisons. Jealousy can imprison a person more than bars. Live for Christ while you can on earth, and then enjoy the rest of your time with Jesus when you leave this place. Go for the win-win. It's definitely a "get out of jail free" card.

Freedom in Accountability

PHILIPPIANS 2:1–18

When accountability groups gained popularity, leaders worked with a list of ten questions to help people in their spiritual lives. The questions dealt with whether or not one made ethical decisions regarding money, how they treated family members, whether they were flirtatious or lustful with the opposite sex, personal health, and how well one maintained a life of prayer and Bible study. The last question in the list of ten was "Have you lied to us on any of your answers today?"[24] That was the one that always got me in trouble. It's always that last question that catches me.

I like to play a game with friends and family to avoid answering a question, which I do by giving a silly answer. For example, my sons would ask when we were going to eat dinner. My response was to say, "Dinnertime." They would press me as to what time dinnertime was, and I would say, "That's when we're going to eat." This back and forth between my sons and me would go on for a few minutes until their mom would tell us to stop and tell the boys what time we were eating.

Another approach was to respond to the question with a question. An example of this would be when asked if I ate the last piece of pie, I would respond with, "What makes you think I would do that?" Quite often, the deflection of topic avoidance or the question for a question would buy me the escape from the truth. Unfortunately, all I did was train those closest to me to ask the last question.

When my family lived in Natchez, there was an unbelievably good

---

[24] https://waynestiles.com/10-accountability-questions-to-grow-your-christian-life/.

mom-and-pop doughnut shop. I became a frequent enough visitor that the mom and pop knew my name, where I worked, and the location of my birthplace. I would go on Saturday mornings and buy a dozen for the boys while they watched cartoons. It was a Waddell's Men's Club pact to let their mom sleep in on those lazy Saturdays. The smell of the sweet and savory fried treats would be more than I could handle on the way home, so I would have a doughnut out of the box. The boys, already understanding the mathematical logic of division, knew that eleven could not be divided by four evenly. So, they would ask where the twelfth doughnut was, and I would respond, "I think the poor lady running the shop has difficulty with counting."

Then they would pose the last question to me, "Did you eat one, Dad?"

No matter my deflective response, they would repeatedly ask the last question until the truth came out. It's always that last question that gets me. So, I decided to fix that final question issue. On the following Saturday journey to the doughnut shop, I got the great idea to buy the dozen in a box but order a couple in a sack to enjoy on the way home. I opened the box and shared with the boys that the evidence indicated I did not open the box and enjoy any doughnuts. My oldest son asked if I had any doughnuts that were not in the box on the way home. I asked him why he would ask me that to avoid giving a direct response. He paused and then asked, "Uh, Dad, why do you have a little bit of glazed sugar on your chin?"

It's always the last question that catches me. When my family moved from Natchez to Springfield, Missouri, we had to go back on one final journey to close the deal on our house. As we left town, I decided to make one more sentimental visit to the doughnut shop. As I opened my car door, the lady owner stuck her head out of the window and screamed, "David Waddell, where have you been hiding?"

When I got back in the car with a dozen sweet treats for our journey home, my wife questioned whether I made more trips than the occasional Saturday run for the boys. I attempted deflection by claiming I was making spiritual trips to see if the couple would want to come to church. She didn't have to ask the last question that time.

Her facial expression of my deflection communicated the same thing. She could see the truth all over my face, despite there being no glazed doughnut sugar on my chin.

I don't recall living in Philippi when Paul gave his cell call, but I must have. So much of what he writes about hits me square in the heart. For example, the second part of his cell call starts with a series of questions about encouragement from Christ, getting comfort from Christ's love, being in fellowship with the Spirit, and whether I have a compassionate heart. I didn't realize there was going to be a pop quiz! At least he didn't ask me that last question as to whether I lied about the first four questions.

Then, as if Paul hadn't picked on me enough, he gave me a list of things to do. He listed a to-do list, such as agreeing with others, loving others, working with others for one purpose, being humble, thinking of others more than myself, looking out for the interests of others, and having the attitude of Christ Jesus.

Ouch.

I heard a line once regarding humility that went like this, "I'm very humble. I'm proud of the humility I have. It's my humility that makes me better than everyone else." The difficulty I have with humility is that I am an attention seeker. I love to be in the center! So, on one of my spontaneous summer tours, I drove to the geographical center of the contiguous United States, located in Lebanon, Kansas. I took a photo to put on Facebook and captioned it, "I may not be the center of the Universe, but right now I'm the center of the United States."

To help me out, Paul gives an example of what it means to be like Christ. Jesus, who had divine privileges, gave them up to humble himself to be a slave for humanity. He died a criminal's death before being elevated to the highest place of honor. The name of Jesus is a name above all other names, and everyone will declare He is Lord.

Then Paul continues with practical things we can do. Live clean, don't complain, be innocent, and shine a bright light in a dark world. Again, with the follow-up responses? Thanks, Paul. OK, I admit I am a complainer. Even when things are good, I can find the one thing that is not and whine about it. Negativity breeds quickly. When I consulted at the Kirby Pines Estates in Memphis, I discovered the tables in the break room were small so that only four people could sit at any particular table. They spread the tables out like that, making it hard to hear the conversation at another table. The human resource director told me this was normal in many places. They set the design of the tables this way so that only three other people would share their influence if one table turned negative.

Paul knew that if I didn't live clean, refrain from complaining, and avoid shining the light of Jesus, there would be no way people would see the difference Jesus has made in my life. Paul concludes this part of his letter by pointing out a couple of people who demonstrate the difference Jesus made in their lives. Paul commends Timothy and Epaphroditus to the people of Philippi in what sounds like a letter of recommendation.

As a sport and recreation administration lecturer, I am often asked to write letters of recommendation for my students. Being blessed with the gift of encouragement, I find it an enjoyable experience to tell others about the greatness of one of my students. It's been a joy to find something in all of them that works its way into a recommendation letter. These letters are a form of networking, which my students also hear a lot about in class. If someone who has credibility tells another about someone they don't know, the credibility extends itself.

As I write this, our world remains in the middle of the coronavirus pandemic. During a Zoom conversation with friends, the topic of recommendation letters came up. One friend stated that when a student asks him to write a recommendation letter, he asks them to write one about themselves to use as a guide. He said he likes to see how the student perceives themselves before writing about how he perceives them. So, I began thinking about how I would write my recommendation letter. Of course, I would have to be truthful because somewhere out there would be a friend to ask me that last question as to whether I lied about anything in the letter.

Any questions for me? We can skip to the last one if you'd like. I'll be sure to wipe the glazed doughnut sugar off my chin before I respond.

There's No I in Team

PHILIPPIANS 2:19–30

My desire to excel in athletics fell short due to an incredible lack of talent. I joke with my classes at the University of Mississippi that I was one of the most important players on the team when I played sports. For example, if the team was down twenty or more points in the last minute of the game, the coach would put me in. I assume it was his confidence in me to score enough to tie or win the game. Likewise, the coach sent me to protect the lead when our team was ahead by twenty or more. While I could never erase a deficit, I can say with pride that no team caught us with me protecting the considerable lead.

The most significant contribution I offered to my teams in youth sports was when chattering was allowed. My father, sitting behind home plate in the stands, claimed he could hear me clearly when I screamed, "Hey batter-batter-batter-batter-swing," from right field. But, of course, a good chatter would include timing the word *swing* just as the pitch is coming into the batter. So, while my team was up to bat, I would scream, "We need a pitcher, not a belly itcher!"

While the video *Sports Highlights of David Waddell* would be a short documentary, I did find success in high school as a part of the speech and debate squad. Those who know me would not be surprised, as I can speak a lot about things I know nothing about. I made the team my junior year. I performed humorous interpretation for the team, which meant I independently shared scenes from different plays or movies. My biggest hit was the PLO (permanent latrine orderly) scene from *No Time for Sergeants*.

In debate, my partner was Dave Lenox. We quickly became known as the Dave and Dave team. During my junior year, I earned my first trophy both in debate and humorous interpretation. It was in my senior year, however, that the entire team found its most tremendous success. Each year, schools were allowed to participate in ten speech and debate tournaments. Each debate team and individual component earned team points for their success by winning a round of debate or scoring high in the individual events. The school would receive additional points by placing high enough wins or scores to make the final rounds. The culmination of the tournament was in awarding a sweepstakes trophy for the school with the most points earned throughout the tournament. My team from Kickapoo High School in Springfield, Missouri, coached by Jack Tuckness, won six sweepstakes out of the ten tournaments, finishing second in the other four.

It was a joy and is an excellent memory to think back on, being a part of such a great team. Six debate teams and a host of individual components all worked together for the team to succeed. Unfortunately, as a debate team, Dave and I were never able to get past the semifinals. In humorous interpretation, a third-place finish was as high as I ever achieved. As I look back, I take more pride in the team's success than the individual trophies my performance obtained.

Part of the training I give students in our outdoor recreation class is the opportunity to lead in team-building games. The purpose of these games is to lessen inhibitions and free people up to work on being better teammates. My favorite is when students lead the other students in a game of human knot. First, the group stands in a circle and reaches into the circle to join hands with someone else. Then the students reach out their other hand and take another student's hand. Then the group attempts to untangle without letting go of each other's hands.

The excitement begins as you see the team strategizing and trying different approaches to undo the human puzzle they have created. Introverted people speak up, and the entire group encourages and praises the least athletic people on the team. Everyone is striving to work together to accomplish the goal. That is the perfect definition of a team. Ecclesiastes 4:9 states, "Two people are better off than one, for they can help each other succeed" (NLT).

One of the greatest professional basketball players was Kareem Abdul-Jabbar, who played for the Milwaukee Bucks and Los Angeles Lakers. Despite the numerous records he broke and the amazing individual menace he was on the court, he realized the necessity of teamwork. He once said, "One man can be a crucial ingredient on a team, but no one man can make a team."[25]

The concept of team has created several clichés people depend on for success, such as "there's no I in team." Another makes an acronym that represents Together Everyone Achieves More. John Maxwell wrote a book titled *Teamwork Makes the Dream Work*, where he is quoted as saying, "Teamwork makes the dream work, but a vision becomes a nightmare when the leader has a big dream and a bad team." [26]

When I look back at my life, I have enjoyed serving with several great teams. However, I sincerely doubt I would have made it to this point without others helping me succeed. Each of those teammates contributed to the team in ways that I could not. I tell the story of Alice Rambin in my second book.

> As we were reminiscing about various youth trips and events, I made a confession to her. "Alice," I said, "I never would have been successful in my work had it not been for you. You provided the details when I simply had my head in a visionary cloud. I'm telling you this because you probably don't know how much you helped me in my years in Natchez."

---

[25] John Maxwell, *Teamwork Makes the Dream Work* (Nashville, TN: Countryman Publishing, 2002).
[26] Maxwell, 2002.

Alice gave a slightly sarcastic grin back at me and said, "Oh yes. I know."[27]

Another previous teammate was John Longworth. Here's the story on him.

> My associate recreation pastor came to my office and praised how visionary I was as a leader. Then he offered to meet with me once a week to discuss the big picture of where I saw the recreation ministry going in this church. Then he volunteered that he could work behind the scenes with the details and help me make the vision a reality. I was amazed how complimented I felt in being told that I was pretty weak in the details of programming events and activities. We were able to accomplish some amazing things because this man didn't care about getting attention as long as the mission of the ministry was being carried out.[28]

Paul points out to his Philippian friends two people on his team who have been very helpful: Timothy and Epaphroditus. These two men were part of Paul's team. Paul first heard of Timothy on his second missionary journey. When he stopped in Lystra, he found Timothy, who had a Jewish mother who was a believer and a Greek father. Paul invited Timothy to join him. Despite all the other aspects of Paul preaching grace in Christ, he decided to have Timothy circumcised to avoid issues with Jewish believers because he had a Greek father. Timothy was with Paul on several efforts from this point on and helped Paul keep in touch with his friends.

Paul shared with his Philippian friends how much Timothy cared for them. Timothy stood out on the team as Paul reported some others were more concerned for themselves. Paul saw Timothy as

---

[27] David Waddell, *Holiday Biblical Characters: Finding My Stories in the Stories of Christmas and Easter* (WestBow Publishing, 2015).
[28] Waddell, 2015.

being like a son to him. Paul trusted Timothy to deliver a message to the Philippian church and to return with a response back to Paul.

Epaphroditus was a messenger for the church and Paul. He was sent by the church when they heard of Paul's great need. He almost died from an illness, but through God's mercy and healing, he survived. Paul takes great joy in having Epaphroditus on the team. He was anxious to send him back to Philippi to comfort the people of the church. Paul made sure they knew Epaphroditus had risked his life for the sake of the Gospel and for ministering to him in place of the Philippians.

Can you imagine being in the human knot game with Paul, Timothy, Epaphroditus, and others under Paul's influence? Now, that would have been an enjoyable team to observe. They won a better version of the sweepstakes trophy. We'll meet their success stories when we get to heaven.

Who are the current teammates in your human knot?

What Is Really Important Here

PHILIPPIANS 3:1–11

I tell my students that I was once associated with the NFL. Of course, they balk and laugh at the idea until I tell them that this NFL was the National Forensic League. I was a part of the speech and debate team during my junior and senior years of high school. The governing body of the tournaments we participated in was the National Forensic League, which changed its name in 2014 to the National Speech and Debate Association. The league awarded points for participating in speech and debate activities. Winning the debate or finishing higher in other events led to more points than losing or merely participating.[29]

During my junior year, the most crucial thing I desired was winning the first trophy in my life. I did not excel in athletics, and during my youth, trophies were not given simply for participation. I played in one championship baseball game with my church's twelve-and-under baseball team, which featured a future professional baseball player, Rick Sutcliffe. Unfortunately, we lost the championship game 13–6. I don't even remember if the team got a trophy.

My debate partner, Dave Lenox, and I finished fourth in the Springfield Parkview High School Tournament, which won us a plaque. I was so proud of that award. It was, at the time, the most important thing I shot for in speech and debate.

During my time in speech and debate, the award from the NFL that I was going after was the Double Ruby for Special Distinction.

---

[29] https://sites.google.com/a/mcsdonline.org/mhsforensics/national-forensics-league.

It became a goal, but more than that, it became my passion. It was of great desire for me to get the Double Ruby. Unfortunately, I fell fifty points short and settled for the Distinction degree and a Single Ruby award.

Life changes what we deem most important. I tell people when I was in high school, all I wanted was to finish and be in college. While I was in college, all I wanted to do was finish and be in seminary. While I was in the seminary, all I wanted to do was finish and be in my first church job. When I finally arrived in that first church job, all I wanted was to be back in high school.

While in my first church, my actual desire was to get to a bigger church. I never seemed to be satisfied where God had me. I always wanted bigger or more. I look back at my life, and whether it was in a career position or a relationship, I seemed to run after the things that weren't all that important to me.

When some people discuss what is important, they refer to the letters after one's name: the more degrees and certifications one has obtained, the more important that person appears to be. When the letters MD follow a name, you know they've done some work to get to that point. In academic circles, the letters signify the path of work one has accomplished. PhD reflects more of an accomplishment than an MA. The letters following the name work off the highest degree and then reverse order by the other degrees. My undergraduate degree is a bachelor of science, while my graduate degree is a master of religious education, making my signature David Waddell MRE BS. To be funny with my students, I add the O for the word *of* in the title when I spell it out on the whiteboard, making the word MORE. The students never put up any argument with that signature.

The church in Philippi was dealing with some of the same difficulties as the other churches when Paul gave his cell call. Legalists were pushing for circumcision to be the sign of being a Christ follower. Paul reminds the Philippians that our reliance has to be on Christ. That is the most crucial thing in our lives. To make the point, Paul runs through the highlights of his résumé. He claims circumcision at the age of eight, member of the Benjamin tribe, member of the

Pharisees, and obedient and zealous enough to persecute the church. He confesses he thought these things were valuable but now sees them all as worthless. In the New Living Translation, Paul refers to his accomplishments as garbage (Philippians 3:8 NLT). In some translations, garbage translates as dung or excrement. Modern slang would have a different take on it, which I'll not share here.

I understand his thinking here. I don't usually lead initial conversations by introducing my baseball or speech and debate successes. I don't deem what was once the most important thing in my life as being all that important anymore. I accidentally left all my speech and debate trophies in the attic of my home in Natchez, Mississippi, when my family and I moved back to Springfield, Missouri. The new homeowners asked my wife what they should do with them, and she instructed them to throw them out. At first, I was upset, but then I realized the trophies were already eighteen years old and had always been in storage for my adult life. The lack of metal doesn't diminish the memory of winning them. So, in a sense, Paul, my accomplishments became garbage!

In the long run, those items helped make me who I am today, but I am not defined or limited by those events. Paul reminds me and the rest of us that God made us right with him by faith. It's not what we have done but, instead, what Christ has done. Paul reminds the Philippians and us that we need to forget the past and set our eyes on the prize of being with Christ Jesus. To Paul, the résumé is not nearly as important as the references.

I used to play a game with religious television stations where I would watch until I heard a preacher with questionable theology. Most of the time, it didn't take long before the mention of the health-wealth-prosperity gospel. One time, playing this game, I caught Joel Osteen, and he said something rather incredible. He said there was a reason, in an automobile, that the rearview mirror is small and the front windshield is large. He continued by saying the design was to spend more time looking ahead than we do looking behind. Jesus told his disciples that it does a farmer no good to look backward while plowing a field.

One of my former students, Johnny Neumann, is now in heaven. He was a nontraditional student coming back to school in his sixties. In 1970–1971, Johnny was an All-American basketball player at Ole Miss and later played in the American Basketball Association and the National Basketball Association. Following his playing career, he coached in international leagues. He sat in my office and introduced himself by all of these accolades in his past. I stared at him and said, "That's good, but what have you done for me lately?"

We then discussed how much influence and impact remained for him to share with the world. Three years later, he graduated. Unfortunately, death came to visit before he could continue his mark on the world. Nevertheless, his fellow students still speak of the humor and encouragement he gave during his time at Ole Miss. He enjoyed his past, but he was even more excited about what was ahead of him.

Paul said it this way in his cell call, "I focus on one thing: Forgetting the past and looking forward to what lies ahead. I press on to reach the end of the race and receive the heavenly prize for which God, through Christ Jesus, is calling us" (Philippians 3:13–14 NLT).

So, what's important to you these days?

Archery, with No Target, Gives One the Shaft

PHILIPPIANS 3:12-21

I grew up admiring the work of Charles Schulz, the creator of the *Peanuts* comic strip. Like many in our world, I identified with Charlie Brown. I admired the comic strip so much that I desired to be a cartoonist when I grew up. I studied the work of other cartoonists in the daily and Sunday papers. My mother is a gifted artist in painting, calligraphy, and pottery. Unfortunately, when I attempted cartooning, I realized the artistry DNA missed me.

I heard about one cartoon that I attributed to Charles Schulz. I have shared this particular cartoon with my classes at Ole Miss to demonstrate the need to set goals. In searching for that cartoon, I discovered it is not a Charles Schulz creation. At this point, let me apologize to numerous students I have led astray.[30]

The cartoon is a *Brother Juniper* cartoon, where the young friar shoots his arrows first and then paints the target around the spot the arrow hit.[31]

When I was in church work, I was responsible for planning the summer camps for our church and community. The first and second graders had a day camp, while third through fifth, sixth through eighth, and ninth through twelfth graders had an overnight camp. In each of these camp settings, archery was one of

---

[30] https://scnforyou.com/the-trick-to-hitting-your-target-every-time-scn-encourager/.
[31] http://brotherjuniper.com/2016/05/its-easy-first-you-shoot-the-arrow/.

the track time activities. On occasion, I would have to step in and teach a session. We used plastic bows, but the arrows came with an actual point rather than the suction cup ones you would buy in a toy department.

Archery served the campers well because the word *sin* literally means missing the mark. Or, in other words, you didn't hit the bull's-eye. So, it was easy to teach the campers that regardless of how poorly or excellently they shot an arrow, God's grace covered them for every time they missed the mark in their lives.

Archery also became my love due to the number of puns one can create with the subject. For example, I quiver at collecting arrows in one container. Or, if an arrow hits someone, they definitely got the shaft.

The topic of archery hit my target thinking for this portion of Paul's cell call to the Philippians. Paul speaks of pressing toward the goal, toward his heavenly prize. In other words, he has painted the target first, and then he shoots his arrows. Paul uses a sports analogy of pressing on to win the race. Whether archery or racing, one sets a goal, then works to achieve that goal.

The international director for the Association of Church Sports and Recreation Ministries (CSRM), P.F. Meyers, closes every email and phone call the same way: *Keep pressing on!* Those on CSRM staff refer to him as the modern-day Paul the apostle, as he is willing to go anywhere to proclaim the love and grace of Jesus. P.F. sets out what he aims to accomplish, and then he goes after it. P.F. paints the target first and then shoots.

Paul, the actual apostle, uses "pressing on" to remind his Philippian friends to strive for perfection in Christ. Paul admits he has yet to achieve perfection, but it remains his goal. The bull's-eye for Paul and his Philippian friends was forgetting the past and seeking what was ahead. Paul's message has so much for us today. I know when I'm driving or walking and my gaze is concentrating on what I've passed rather than what I'm approaching, I tend to veer off my path. The car I drive now has a warning sound when I slide over to one side of the road or the other. If I stare out a side window or my rearview mirror, the signal beeps to remind me to look ahead and adjust my target's aim.

Paul then addresses the need to stay true to the correct pattern of living. He tells his friends in this cell call to pattern their lives after his example. There were those in Philippi who talked a good game, but they were leading people to destruction. These people were shooting the arrow first, then painting the target.

The next part of Paul's cell call is one of those "stepping on my toes" moments. In a recent interview with Dan Steuer on the Finish Last podcast, we discussed various places around the United States to get the best barbecue. First, I told Dan I was born and raised in Kansas City, Missouri, known for barbecue. Next, I lived eight years in Texas, which is known for barbecue. Finally, twenty-four years of my life have been in the Memphis, Tennessee, area known for, you guessed it, barbecue. I commented that my life might have more of a calling to barbecue than it does to ministry and academia.[32]

Paul talks about the false teachers and that their god is their appetite. Ouch, Paul. There's a phrase that hits me as much as the appetite god, which is "Do you eat to live or live to eat?" I have to confess that certain foods create the live-to-eat scenario. If I know I have a particular meal planned, I set my aim and target that day. I have set fasting as my target at certain times in my life to make sure barbecue, nachos, and cheeseburgers were not my God. Now, going without my favorite foods makes me quiver.

Paul also explains how these false teachers brag about shameful things. I remember a joke where a preacher called in sick one Sunday morning to drive over to the next county and get in a round of golf. St. Peter pointed out the preacher on the golf course to God and asked what kind of judgment the Almighty would dispense. The preacher teed off on a par five hole, and his drive flew in the air and landed in the middle of the fairway. A squirrel picked up the ball and started running toward the woods. The talons of a mighty eagle picked up the squirrel and flew toward the green. At the edge of the green, the

---

[32] https://open.spotify.com/episode/5Ya9TKgWaKEeKrNln3gkob.

eagle dropped the squirrel, and the force of the rodent hitting the ground made it lose the golf ball, which rolled into the cup for a hole in one.

St. Peter, a little upset, asked God why he allowed a church-skipping pastor to get such a fantastic hole-in-one, and God said, "Who is he going to tell?"

I've done some sinful and dumb stuff in my life where God was asking me the same question. I shared some of these with a counselor once, and he asked, in so many words, why I would set a target for something I couldn't tell anyone when I hit the bull's-eye. The false teachers in Philippi were bragging about similar shameful things the rest of us wouldn't dare reveal.

Paul closes this bit of his cell call to remind us that our home is in heaven, where our mortal bodies transform into glorious bodies like Christ.

What target are you shooting at presently? Where's your aim? Or are you shooting arrows first and painting the target later? Can you tell us about it later?

Let's pick a worthy target and fire away. That way, we can make our point without giving someone the shaft.

Don't Worry. Be Happy.

PHILIPPIANS 4:2–9

It's rather unfortunate that in the five churches I served on staff, three of them split during my tenure, one split later, and one is no longer in existence. How do I put that on my ministry résumé? The split in the first church was over the effectiveness of the current pastor, led by supporters of the former pastor. The night I announced my resignation to move to another church, the two other staff members resigned without a new place of service lined up. Then someone moved for the pastor to resign. The motion received a second, and a heated discussion making seasoned politicians look amateurish took place. Finally, the vote on the pastor's resignation was taken and defeated.

The second split resulted as collateral damage in the conservative versus moderate battle in the Southern Baptist Convention. One of my dear friends and a former professor at Missouri State University asked where I stood on the issues. I told her, with a smirk on my face, I was on the fence. She shared I couldn't stay on the fence. I told her, "Oh, not only can I stay on the fence, I have a pillow to keep the chain-link wires from poking me in the bottom." The primary component of the fight, and please know this still sounds silly to me, was an argument about how we would tell the world about Jesus. I was proud of my oldest son, who, at age fourteen, questioned in a business meeting why we were arguing so terribly. I tried to explain it to him later, only later to admit my ignorance of the situation.

The third came about from a staff-led effort to move the church into an elder-led leadership style. The church was a longtime traditional Southern Baptist Church that operated under a deacon and committee government structure. Monthly business meetings tended to get rather dull until the announcement of a move to an elder structure. I joked with others that we sounded like that old credit card commercial bragging on being a member since a particular year. People would introduce themselves as members for so many years to give them more credibility than some "rookie" church members. Both sides drew battle lines, and the conversations in the hallways and parking lots became "exciting." Unfortunately, my youngest son questioned the topic, like his older brother years before, and became branded as a troublemaker.

The pastor in the first church survived and served that church many more years, up until his retirement. Reconciliation took place as many of the "scorned" former members returned to the church. The second church had several members leave to attend like-minded churches in the area. While still effective in ministry, the church has never returned to the level of attendance or influence they once knew. The third church, which began as a megachurch, split off to create a new church and bolster the attendance of other churches in the area. While some of their ministries ceased to exist, the church remains a strong influence in their community. Thankfully, all three survived my "splitting giftedness."

I wish these were rare occurrences, but they are not. Two sides of an idea, a proposal, or current leadership effectiveness tend to divide churches. While the church is full of saints, the sinfulness of wanting to be right gets in the way of church unity. The problem I've discovered in church fights is that both sides feel they are in the middle of God's will and the other side is serving Satan. It's pretty rare where that is the truth in any case. I've never heard of a church splitting over any dispute where one side wanted to support a sinful, immoral, or illegal activity. Most of the conflicts in the church, in my understanding, deal with money and power. It's usually about who gets to call the shots and who controls the use of the money.

Some church disputes even make their way into the judicial system in the United States. One group in the church sues the other group so that a judge can decide who is right. Paul referred to this notion in an earlier letter he wrote to the church in Corinth, "When one of you has a dispute with another believer, how dare you file a lawsuit and ask a secular court to decide the matter instead of taking it to other believers!" (1 Corinthians 6:1 NLT). Followers of Jesus are supposed to be able to work things out among themselves.

Another reason the first-century letter from a prisoner has a message for us today is that the church in Philippi was dealing with this same kind of issue. Paul appealed to two women in some sort of disagreement that was hurting the church's ministry. Eudia and Syntyche were very helpful to Paul and others in spreading the Good News of Christ. The fact that Paul mentions it in his cell call means it must have been affecting the church's work.

I understand Paul's concern. How do we preach a message of love when we can't even get along with one another? Paul may have recalled the effect his split with Barnabus caused earlier in his life (Acts 15: 36–41). The culture seems to feed off the fact that there is so much infighting among Christians. Fortunately, Paul gives us a remedy in the next part of his cell call, which is to be full of God's joy.

Paul believed this so much he pulled the repetition trick and said, "I say it again—rejoice!" (Philippians 4:4 NLT). Continuing this thought, Paul says, "Don't worry about anything, but instead pray about everything" (Philippians 4:6 NLT). In other words, "Don't worry. Be happy!"

The phrase "Don't worry, be happy" was started by the Indian mystic Meher Baba, who used the expression when messaging people in the West. Bobby McFerrin saw the phrase on a poster and thought it was "a pretty neat philosophy in four words."[33] So in 1988, McFerrin wrote a famous song using that phrase. The song is a perfect message for people who are finding a lot going wrong in their lives. Here are some of the lyrics:

---

[33] https://www.songfacts.com/facts/bobby-mcferrin/dont-worry-be-happy.

> Here's a little song I wrote
> You might want to sing it note for note
> Don't worry, be happy
> In every life we have some trouble
> But when you worry you make it double
> Don't worry, be happy
> Don't worry, be happy now[34]

Paul reminds his Philippian friends that worry gets nothing done and that they should concentrate on telling God what they need and thanking Him for all He's done in their lives. The result is peace beyond all understanding.

The best way to not worry and be happy, which will minimize any possibility of an Euodia and Syntyche fight in the church, is to concentrate our minds on what is true, honorable, right, pure, lovely, and admirable (Philippians 4:8). When a thought enters my mind that is none of the above, I like to establish what I call the "purple frog theory." I can't help what thoughts enter my mind, but I can control how long they stay there. I've discovered if I am harboring ugly or impure thoughts about someone or a situation, I can't simply not think about it. I have to replace the thought with another thought to take over my mind. In other words, if I try not to think about a pink elephant, I'll think about it until I replace it with a purple frog. Therefore, when my mind turns to ugliness or other sinful thoughts, I replace them with something pure, true, honorable, and so on.

If we think about these good things and remember all the other reminders from Paul's cell call, we will recognize God's peace so much more.

Feel like fighting? Replace that thought with a purple frog. In other words, "Don't worry. Be happy."

---

[34] https://www.azlyrics.com/lyrics/bobbymcferrin/dontworrybehappy.html.

The State in Which I Live

PHILIPPIANS 4:10–20

I entered the flower shop to buy some yellow daisies and have them delivered them to a lady whose affection I was trying to win. Then I saw that my friend Smitty, who helped his mom operate the floral shop, was on the phone. I knew him best from his time at Chick-fil-A, serving me chicken biscuits with extra butter. He was also friends with the football player who introduced me to Conecuh sausage on a Camp Leadership class outing. So, I liked him a lot.

My friend hung up the phone and asked me what I had planned over the weekend. I told him that I didn't have much planned other than to help my son move from one house to another in Memphis. I inquired of him as to why he was asking. He told me he had two tickets to the College World Series in Omaha, Nebraska, but didn't have a way to get there. I told him how ironic that was since I had a way to get there but had no tickets.

With my son's permission to skip the moving assistance, I left at four thirty the next morning and picked Smitty up, and we were off to Omaha. Along the way, I introduced him to my all-time favorite cheeseburger at HiBoy's in Independence, Missouri. Ole Miss had lost once in the tournament, which meant one more loss and they were out. Smitty and I got to town in time to see Ole Miss beat Texas Tech. We sat in front of a man who came to the game dressed as Elvis. Because of his costume, our entire section appeared several times on ESPN. Sitting next to me were two gorgeous ladies with whom I was involved in a conversation. Because of the Elvis impersonator, the ladies and I made several television appearances when the network showed Elvis in the crowd.

The game rained out the next night, so Smitty and I went to a nearby place for dinner. While there, a couple of ladies were intrigued by my accent and struck up a conversation. I had my photo taken with both and posted it on Facebook. One of my friends commented on the picture by asking how I got four different women to hang out with me on two separate nights.

My reply was "It's my Missouri-Texas-Tennessee-Mississippi accent. It attracts ladies everywhere except Missouri, Texas, Tennessee, and Mississippi."

In my life, I have had the joy of living in four different states. During those years, I have adopted certain accents or statements from each place. My accent is so mixed up that when I go home to Missouri, they don't think I'm from that state. On the other hand, when I speak in Mississippi, where I've lived the past fifteen years and twenty-one overall, they tell me the same thing as my Missouri friends.

I'm a man without a home! On the journey home, Smitty and I picked up a friend who needed a ride home. In northern Missouri, we encountered a group of students with an old truck and camper combination stranded on the side of the road. We suspicioned the group partook of some mind-altering activities, as we determined they must be from the state of confusion. So, we took off, unable to assist them. They refused our offer to send help back to the camper.

Being a barbecue fan, I have wondered if that has not been my overall calling in life. First, I was born in the Kansas City, Missouri area, which is famous for barbecue. Then I lived eight years in Texas, which is known for barbecue. Finally, I have lived twenty-three years in or near Memphis, which is also known for barbecue. I suppose my next move will be to the Carolinas, as they are the remaining place for barbecue reputation.

It's interesting to hear how people declare they couldn't be happy living anywhere else. I have students who love the Oxford community enough to take whatever job is available in the area rather than seek employment in the area of their degree elsewhere. But, on the other hand, I've heard people say things like, "There's no way I could live in New York City." Or "I couldn't handle the cold weather of the North."

A popular meme circulates, claiming, "Say what you will about the South, but no one retires and moves north." More than likely, at retirement, I will prove the meme wrong and move north. Contentment is more of an attitude than it is a financial status or geographical place.

Regardless of which state I have lived in, I have found a comfort level in being there. I used to joke about Paul's statement in his cell call to the Philippians where he says, "Not that I speak in respect to lack for I have learned in whatever *state* I am, to be content in it" (Philippians 4:11 World English Bible, emphasis mine). Of course, I like to take the first part out of context and relate it to my homes in Missouri, Texas, Tennessee, and Mississippi.

Paul describes what the state of contentment looked like when he encouraged the Philippians near the end of his cell call. He reminded them that prayer is more effective than worry, constantly being full of joy and fixing one's mind on the important stuff that is true, honorable, right, pure, lovely, and admirable.

When visiting other places, I remember the phrase "It's a nice place to visit, but I wouldn't want to live there." This statement expresses my life in the state of contentment. I feel that I live part-time in the state of contentment or that I'm just an occasional visitor. I feel as though I'm content; however, if I had just three more things in life, I could be really content. But then I realize I've just defied the definition of contentment. Besides the states mentioned above, here are some other states where I have lived:

> *The state of covetousness.* There have been times when I wanted a wife like someone else had, a house that someone else owned, or a car that was better than a fifty-fifty chance of starting. The grass always seems greener on the other side of the fence.

The state of need. At numerous times in my life, I found I was in need. During my time in the seminary, a celebration consisted of the two-dollar meal deal at Church's Fried Chicken across the street from our duplex. I've been in situations where I needed a new job or a salary increase. Other times, I have desired a new relationship or the mending of a current one. When I started writing, I needed a publisher.

The state of thanks. God has been good to me through the times of covetousness and need. God has shown me contentment and has always met my needs. I'm fortunate that I've never been without a job during my adult life. In addition, I feel blessed that God has given me relationships where I have been loved unconditionally.

Paul includes a word of thanks for the financial assistance the Philippian people gave. Paul explains he's not looking for more money but instead shares he has all he needs, which must be the state of being cared for. He declares the same God that took care of him will also take care of the Philippians. That same God will also take care of us.

The cell call concludes as all good communication should, with Paul's final greetings. I'll conclude this chapter with the same. Thank you for your encouragement and support and for reading my writing about practical theology and taking the Bible personally. I pray the words will continue to bless you, in whatever state you reside, as you see yourself as a Philippian to whom Paul wrote.

PAUL'S LETTER TO THE
COLOSSIANS

The city of Colossae was one hundred miles east of Ephesus, in the Lycus River Valley, which is now modern-day Turkey. It sat on the Persian Royal Road that ran between Ephesus and Sardis.[35]

A general belief was that Epaphras heard Paul preach elsewhere and started the Colossian church. However, heresy problems Epaphras was facing in his church led him to seek out Paul. Paul's letter aimed at encouraging the Christian community and protecting them from false teaching.[36]

Paul dealt with heresy by reminding the church of its doctrine and its responsibility to one another in the church and the family.[37]

---

[35] Thompsons, p. 1540.
[36] http://www.jesuswalk.com/colossians/0_intro.htm.
[37] https://www.theologyofwork.org/new-testament/colossians-philemon/introduction-to-colossians-and-philemon/background-on-colossae-and-the-colossians.

Good News or Good News

Colossians 1:1–14

The waiting was over—nine long months awaiting our firstborn child. Please note, I understand the nine months were longer in many ways for the soon-to-be mom than they were for me. First, we opted to wait until the little rascal made their entry into the world before finding out if it was a he or a she. Then, when the due date passed with no child, the doctor wanted to wait it out even more. You can imagine how frustrating this was for the soon-to-be mom. Then, more waiting until finally the doctor gave a "drop date" to induce labor if the child had yet to make their appearance.

Of course, we chose names for both genders. If memory serves me correctly, Jennifer Diane if the baby was a girl, and James David Junior if it was a boy. The doctor induced labor, and I was off with all the coaching techniques learned in our Lamaze classes. However, I realized that if one approaches his pregnant wife's face up close to help her with breathing techniques, one should not have a tuna fish sandwich for lunch.

Hours of unimaginable pain later, our son was born. My memory was correct on his name. During one of the well-baby checks, the doctor discovered an abnormality in James's heart rate. They thought it might be a hole in the heart. The pediatrician referred us to the experts in Houston, Texas, who discovered a valve situation. It wasn't nearly as bad as first expected.

"The good news is you have a son. The bad news is there's a problem with his heart. The good news is it isn't as bad as first diagnosed. The bad news is we have to monitor the situation closely and carefully." The bad news was we wondered if the little guy could fight through this. The good news was he was active in all sorts of youth sports. The bad news was my son entered the world with one strike at-bat. The good news is he is a full-grown man, married, with five children of his own.

Years later, I was playing this son in one of our classic Driveway Basketball League games. The league consisted of him versus me in a best two out of three games to ten points. When we started, I could beat him with relative ease. However, after he grew to be five inches taller than me and developed a strong back and chest, I found it more challenging to win. He won the first game on this day, and I noticed I was more out of breath than usual. Nevertheless, I won the second game before he closed me out in the third. I blamed the breathlessness on my ongoing sinus difficulties and being out of shape.

Later that week, I planned to go with my wife to the Rec Lab, an annual church recreation conference hosted by Lifeway Christian Resources of the Southern Baptist Convention in Orlando, Florida. This year's journey would be the first time in our marriage that she would attend this conference with me. Unfortunately, the day after the basketball games with James, I coughed up some blood and figured this sinus stuff would irritate me during the conference, so I went to see my doctor. Sadly, he discovered an abnormality in my heart rate and made an immediate appointment for me with a cardiologist. Somehow, a viral infection had hit my heart and caused a condition called atrial fibrillation, or A-fib for short. Defined, it's half of the heart beating regularly, and in laymen's terms, the other half is shaking in place.

A sidenote on A-fib. The church's worship pastor asked me to explain what A-fib was, and I asked him if he ever observed me trying to clap in rhythm during worship songs. He responded that he understood the diagnosis immediately.

While in the hospital, my oldest son came to see me, and I pointed out that a "half-hearted old man" was able to beat this healthy college student in one out of three games the day before the diagnosis. The humor of the moment no doubt helped the healing process.

The good news is you extended your son to three games. The bad news is the reason you are so winded is that your heart is hurting. The good news is your wife will go to her first Rec Lab conference with you. The bad news is the two of you are going to the hospital instead.

Our world is full of such paradoxes. For example, the "good news and bad news" dichotomy plays itself out numerous times in our lives. So, when I hear "I have good news and bad news. Which do you want first?" I always opt for the bad news first to have something to look forward to and end on a good note. Ironically, there has been research into this very subject. Angela M. Legg and Kate Sweeny compiled research to determine which news, good or bad, people opt for first. In the study, it was determined, "Most people prefer to begin with a loss or negative outcome and ultimately end with a gain or positive outcome, rather than the reverse."[38]

I like how Paul started his cell call to his Colossian friends. It's not a good news–bad news situation. Instead, Paul begins with what I would call an "I have good news and good news. Which one do you want first?"

After an initial greeting, Paul goes into the good news of hearing about the faith in Christ and the love of others that everyone was experiencing. He speaks of their hope and expectation after hearing the, wait for it, Good News. The good news about the Good News (translated Gospel in many places) is that it is worldwide and changing lives.

The good news is the Colossians first heard of the Good News from a beloved coworker, Epaphras. The good news is Epaphras was keeping Paul informed of what the Colossians were doing with the Good News. Paul continues with the good news that the Good News has motivated him and others to pray for their friends, that they may gain more wisdom and understanding of the Good News. The prayer

---

[38] Do, Rupert, & Wolford 2008; Ross & Simonson 1991; "Do You Want the Good News or the Bad News First? The Nature and Consequences of News Order Preferences," *Personality and Social Psychology Bulletin* 40, no. 3 (2014): 279–288.

is also so the Colossians will have the good news of producing good fruit with the Good News.

Finally, Paul closes out this part of his cell call to communicate that the good news is God rescued us from our darkness into the kingdom of Christ, who, through the Good News, purchased our freedom and forgave us of our sins.

Thank you, Paul. The darkest part of my life occurred early this century when hidden sin made itself known. The revelation immediately led to my resignation from ministry leadership and eventually led to my divorce. However, the good news is that the Good News allowed for my restoration and reclamation. I did leave church work, but the path led to a teaching position in my field at the University of Mississippi. I did end up divorced; however, we remain friends, and my sons have renewed their relationships with me. The good news about my mess-ups is that there's no denying the Good News of God's grace and love. If I had not gone through all of that, I would not be writing these stories for your enjoyment, enlightenment, and edification. This topic reminds me of a meme I once saw on social media that said something like this, "When God put a calling in your life, He already factored in your bad choices."[39]

I like Paul's good news and Good News option.

---

[39] https://makeameme.org/meme/when-god-put. *Author exchanged one word for more appropriate word in quote.

Mirror Image
Colossians 1:15–23

I have a charcoal drawing that hangs on a wall next to my entry into the kitchen. My mother, a gifted artist, drew it a few years before my dad passed away. When I walk by and see it, I have to remind myself it's a picture of my father, Wes Waddell, and not me looking in a mirror. So, let me say, with a sense of false humility and modesty, I'm glad Dad was handsome because I look just like him.

A few years ago, I made one of my spontaneous summer trips and visited my aunt Ruth in Missouri. She was Dad's older sister and the only one from Dad's immediate family who was still with us. Aunt Ruth had Alzheimer's, so my cousin, Barbara, said she might not recognize me. I entered her room with Barbara, and the first thing out of Aunt Ruth's mouth was "You look like Wes."

I might as well be a mirror image of my father.

I also got Dad's temperament. Dad was so levelheaded that I don't recall him losing his temper much. Rarely did he ever scream or raise his voice. Even in doling out punishment and consequences, he was calm in his demeanor. If I was in trouble and required to sit in the corner or get a swat on the backside, Dad would calmly ask if I knew why I was getting punished. Then he would calmly assign the consequence. More times than not, I disciplined my children the same way. I have had difficulty in some relationships because of the way I express my anger. One lady insisted that I express my emotions about a troubling situation. I stated my comment in an overly calm voice: "I am mad."

It gets worse. I sound like my dad as well. Not in the Missouri-Texas-Tennessee-Mississippi accent that I've picked up through life as much as in the things I say. Dad was known to be very kind to servers in restaurants, to the point he'd carry on a conversation as if he knew the person. He'd do the same thing at checkout counters of stores. I portray the same behavior now, and my friends ask why I personalize every visit. I admit I am a mirror image of my father. An insurance company runs television advertisements about new homeowners becoming like their parents. I find the commercials funny, as that is exactly what I have become. I got to the point that I stopped counting the number of times I said something that sounded just like Dad. My sons point out and tease me with how much of my go-to comments are copied and pasted directly from my father. When I taught them to drive, I would tell them to assume that every other driver on the road was a complete moron. It was a phrase my father used in teaching his sons to drive. My middle son, in a mirror image, exhibiting the quick wit that was transferred to him through me from my dad, asked, "Dad, if I'm driving Mom's car and you're driving your car at the same time, does that mean you're a complete moron?"

I admit moments of wittiness like these make me proud of my children. So, I replied, "Yes, son. Yes, it does."

The similarities don't stop with Dad. My younger brother, Mark, and I were frequently mistaken for each other in the church we attended. The people our age never got it wrong, but the adults in the church couldn't keep us straight. Mark and I never understood the confusion, as we didn't look that much alike. As Mark would point out, he was the good-looking one. That same church hosted a reunion a few years ago of all the youth groups from the 1970s and 1980s. I was able to attend, but Mark was not. During a Saturday-afternoon meeting, one of the adults came in and greeted me, "Hello, Mark." I suppose I can't get away from the mirror image of family similarities. Some things go on from generation to generation. People tell my middle son to watch how I age because people see the exact mirror image in him. I never met my great-grandfathers. I can read stories and genealogies about them, but I did not know them. Yet I imagine a lot of my looks and personality came from their behaviors and their DNA. I am a mirror reflection of all the Waddell and Facemire kin who lived long before me.

Paul shares with us the beauty of this look-alike feature in life beyond the immediate family. He begins his cell call to the church at Colossae by reaffirming who they are in Christ Jesus. Paul first gives a word of thanks for the way the church is telling others about Jesus. Next, he commends them for spreading the Gospel all over the world. Paul also thanks God for the amazing rescue He provided us from the eternal consequences of our sin. Finally, Paul reminds the Colossians that they share in the inheritance of the Father.

Then, in turn, Paul talks of how Jesus is the image of God personified for us on earth. In the way I see myself in my father, Paul describes Jesus in terms of His Father. Paul calls Him "the visible image of the invisible God" (Colossians 1:15a NLT). Jesus, he points out, was there from the beginning and holds all creation together. Paul relates the shedding of Christ's blood as the means of peace between heaven and earth. Then the revelation of beauty comes in verse 22, "Yet now he has reconciled you to himself through the death of Christ in his physical body. As a result, he has brought you into his own presence, and you are holy and blameless as you stand before him without a single fault" (Colossians 1:22 NLT).

Aunt Ruth looked at me and saw her brother and my father. Adults at First Baptist Church in Springfield, Missouri, looked at me and saw Mark. God, through Jesus's death and resurrection, looks at me and sees Jesus. I am holy and without blame. This principle is one of the hardest for some people to believe. It comes about by people's choice to believe we continue to be sinners, scum, and scalawags, even in our state of salvation.

I suppose this mindset comes about because people want to remember the amazing sacrifice Christ made for us when we were sinners, scum, and scalawags. We look in the mirror and see the inner thoughts and outward actions that put us in trouble. We can't see the holy because we're concentrating on the wrong reflection. I look at the charcoal drawing of Dad, and I see me. I need to look in the mirror of my life and see Jesus. To see anything else minimizes the cost Christ paid for me. Paul is clear, as is the Gospel, that Christ has made us a mirror image of our Father.

I find it comical how people can see sights such as mountains, oceanside beaches, and beautiful sunsets and sunrises and praise the Creator of those beautiful sights. But then they look in the mirror and concentrate on the inadequacies of their creation. So, in a backward way of encouraging others, I sometimes ask a person if they ever look in the mirror and say, "Way to go, God! I'm looking good!"

When they laugh and say no, I remind them that they should. God made us in His image, and we are the mirror reflection of Jesus. So, when we look in the mirror and see Jesus, we also see ourselves in light of how God looks at us. We are His beautiful creation. The writer of Psalm 8 said it this way: "When I look at the night sky and see the work of your fingers—the moon and the stars you set in place—what are mere mortals that you should think about them, human beings that you should care for them? Yet you made them only a little lower than God and crowned them with glory and honor" (Psalm 8:3–5 NLT).

Paul closes this section of the letter encouraging the Colossians to continue telling the story and presenting others to God in the perfection of Jesus. Carry a mirror with you and show them the reflection of Christ.

Look in the mirror. See Jesus? You should. Oh, and by the way, you're looking good!

My Pain—Your Gain

Colossians 1:24–29

I couldn't help but overhear the conversation. A gentleman with a certain amount of influence in the church complained about his grandson needing to be on a different baseball team in the church's recreation program. My associate recreation pastor tried to communicate why the team selection occurred the way it did, but the man was looking for a different answer. Finally, the gentleman told my colleague that he should bend to his will, in so many words. After all, he pointed out that he paid this man's salary through his tithes and gifts to the church.

My associate then said, "Is that how it works? Well, I tithe, too, which makes me my own boss. So, I'm giving myself the rest of the day off."

With that, he left the man standing by himself in his office. He attempted to play me as well, but when he saw that neither of us would budge, he angrily left the recreation center office.

The manipulation of the "I pay your salary" is one of the jokes, teasers, and insults pastors and ministers get to put up with as church staff members. Another is how pastors and ministers only have to work one day a week. So, when I would hear that, I would turn it on people and say, "That may be true, but think about it this way. When we take a week of vacation, we only get one day off."

Since I'm no longer in a church position, I feel a bit of freedom to discuss the abuses your church's paid staff must deal with by serving the church. You may want to take a break from reading as I go into this rant. While you're breaking, grab some cheese and crackers. It'll go well with my upcoming serving of whine.

Most of your pastoral staff receive nowhere near the salary as their level of education would dictate in other fields. The church's response to that issue is that a calling into ministry should end any worldly desires about money. Unfortunately, this issue usually creates a situation where the minister's spouse needs a job to keep the family financially afloat.

I had one church offer me an increase in salary to support my wife working as a stay-at-home mom. The pay increase would go away if she worked outside the home for any reason. I turned down the increase by stating I was either worth a raise on my own merits, or not, but not so others could dictate how my family lived. I didn't get the salary increase. I guess my merits didn't merit the increase.

Another situation for pastors is the scheduling of vacations. There are policies as to how many Sundays a pastor can take for vacation days in many churches. Unfortunately, vacation for vocational ministers isn't the same as for others. They can't extend a vacation by using weekends because Sunday is a workday. I realize other occupations, such as health care, caregiving, and retail, are under the same weekend limitations, so please excuse my whining just a bit more.

My heart hurts, especially for pastors and ministers perceived as the "lower part" of the organizational chart. The salary levels for staff members responsible for children, teenagers, or the sports and recreation ministries indicate they are less critical as the "top rung" of senior pastors, worship leaders, and administrators. Yet these people work as hard or harder as those at the top. Often, they put in an equal or greater number of hours to their work. These are the folks who appear in all the Sunday and Wednesday activities of the church and the Friday-night skate parties, overnight lock-ins, and all-day Saturday sports leagues. On top of these additional days, there is a requirement, by being on staff, to be present for any other all-church events.

My former wife and I had a tradition of not buying anniversary gifts for each other. Instead, we invested the money to travel and tour different places around the country. We visited Washington, DC,

Philadelphia, Pennsylvania, Mackinaw Island, Michigan, and other sites. One year, we had the plans set and airline tickets purchased when another staff member, one of the "top rung" ministers, planned a men's retreat with the topic of "Becoming a Better Husband." I was asked in a staff meeting if I was going to attend. I shared my inability as I had already scheduled vacation for those days.

He insisted by wondering what the rest of the church might say if I were to miss the men's event. I couldn't help but get sarcastic by saying, "So, I end up being a bad husband by canceling an anniversary trip with my wife so that I can attend a retreat to learn how to be a better husband."

I didn't go and never heard that anyone wondered why I wasn't there.

When I left church work, I imagined it wouldn't be that difficult to find secular employment. After all, I had been in charge of a large recreation facility and a baseball/softball complex. With revenues, budget money, and expenditures, I was responsible for handling well over five hundred thousand dollars a year. In its heyday, I had a paid staff of eight full-time and fifteen part-time employees. Add to that over three hundred volunteers throughout the year. Indeed, that should qualify me for some high-level leadership position in the secular world. Am I wrong here?

I was wrong. My imagination was way off. No one respected the work in the church the same way they would for a public recreation program. I struggled through six different jobs in three years before landing on my feet at the University of Mississippi. But, again, this is no different than what others have dealt with in various occupations. Oddly enough, one of the six jobs was helping people transition from one career path to another. It was working there that I found the advertisement for the Ole Miss position, which I still hold fifteen years later.

I'll end my rant with that. But, of course, the abuse my pastor and minister friends receive is nowhere near what Paul put up with during his ministry. In the second letter Paul wrote to the church in Corinth, he went through some of the torture he was given to share God's love and grace with others.

> I have worked harder, been put in prison more often, been whipped times without number, and faced death again and again. Five different times the Jewish leaders gave me thirty-nine lashes. Three times I was beaten with rods. Once I was stoned. Three times I was shipwrecked. Once I spent a whole night and a day adrift at sea. I have traveled on many long journeys. I have faced danger from rivers and from robbers. I have faced danger from my own people, the Jews, as well as from the Gentiles. I have faced danger in the cities, in the deserts, and on the seas. And I have faced danger from men who claim to be believers but are not. I have worked hard and long, enduring many sleepless nights. I have been hungry and thirsty and have often gone without food. I have shivered in the cold, without enough clothing to keep me warm. (2 Corinthians 11: 23b–27, NLT)

OK, so Paul's ordeals are not quite like having to be sarcastic about additional work on Saturday or lacking in qualifications for secular work. With all of that on Paul's résumé, he tells his Colossian friends, the suffering was worth it so that he could share the message of Christ with people like them. Paul keeps working so that others can be made perfect in God's eyes through Christ. Paul closes by saying that he puts up with the hardships so others can hear of Christ's mighty power.

Do you know what my pastor and minister friends will tell you, other than on horrible days? They'd say it's worth dealing with less money, long hours, and more trouble to get the opportunity to help change lives. The calling God gave them is real, and somehow, they figure out how to make ends meet. But, on the other hand, I'd be remiss not to offer the idea that we should revisit the church's budget and take care of our church staff better.

Well, that's enough work for me today. I think I'll give myself the rest of the week off.

A New Hope
Colossians 2:1-5

This part of Paul's cell call title is the same as the original *Star Wars: Episode IV*. It is a story of a functioning republic civilization until a power-hungry person desired to rule it all. Little by little, the soon-to-be emperor misled the galaxy, lied to its leaders, and established hate among the people toward the protecting body known as Jedi Knights.

An entire galaxy goes from a shared responsibility government to a dictatorship with what Queen Padme described as, "So, this is how liberty dies, with thunderous applause."[40]

To think, all it took was some concerted conspiracy communications to direct an entire crowd in a different direction. The Pharisees used a similar technique in turning a Jesus-loving crowd into a mob screaming for His crucifixion.

The topic of conspiracy theories reminds me of a humorous experience in my life. Before the pandemic of 2020–2021, I traveled a good bit. I called many of my trips a spontaneous journey because I made up the destinations and rest stops as I went. I've seen the world's largest ball of twine in Cawker City, Kansas. Did you know they allow people to tie new strands of twine to make the ball even larger? Unfortunately, I didn't have any twine with me and therefore missed my part of being recorded in social media history. I have visited the historical sites of our early history and discovered that some of the legends I believed about my heroes, such as Davy Crockett and Daniel

---

[40] https://scatteredquotes.com/liberty-dies-thunderous-applause/.

Boone, were more embellishment than evidence. I learned on many of these journeys that legends often grow faster than the truth. I further learned that some of our early leaders used conspiracy theories to garner strength for our upcoming revolution against Britain.[41]

One planned journey was in July 2019 to visit my friend Lewis DeCarlo in Huntsville, Alabama, on the weekend celebrating the fiftieth anniversary of man's first steps on the moon on July 20, 1969. I arrived Friday afternoon, as there were festivities downtown that evening and a massive concert at the Space Center. Lewis was doing some work around his church, and I had the opportunity to meet his pastor, Tim Milner, a Huntsville native. I jokingly told Tim that I was glad to be a part of the anniversary celebration, as I had been to the place in Arizona where they filmed the moon landing.

Tim laughed and then commented, "No. Don't use that joke tonight. People around here don't take well to that conspiracy theory."

People who worked for NASA, as well as others, know we landed on the moon. Yet, a few stories with a different ending, and some doubt their senses. The engineers and scientists in the Space Center were part of the team who designed all the outer space travel in those days. I can imagine how a family member would take a conspiracy joke somewhat seriously since their moms, dads, uncles, aunts, or grandparents invested sweat and blood equity into the process.

We live in a day where the term *conspiracy theory* is everyday news. A search on Google created 78,200,000 entries. A few that pop up regularly in conversations are the John F. Kennedy and Martin Luther King Jr. assassinations, Area 51 and alien attacks, Bigfoot sightings, Elvis Presley being alive, crop circles, and various unidentified flying objects (UFO). In recent news, there are all sorts of conspiracies around the presidential election and a group known as Q'Anon. But, surprisingly enough, there are still people who believe the world is flat. As I read on social media, "There are flat-Earth believers all around the globe."

---

[41] https://what-when-how.com/conspiracy-theories-in-american-history/american-revolution/.

Like a good practical joke, the difficulty with most conspiracy theories is there's an element of truth or a desired truth in the conspiracy theory. Something in the conspiracy theory is believable enough that the rest of the theory is acceptable to a person. Our human condition desires to know the truth about everything. I, for one, am glad God doesn't reveal the future to me. I fight Him enough in the present; I can't imagine the steps I'd take to prove Him wrong with my future.

I work with a man who enjoys setting up what I call conspiracy pranks. He shares something with me that has enough truth that I buy it as truth and start a campaign against it. I was gullible several times before realizing when he told me something, I should divide it by seven before proceeding with the action. However, a few years ago, he told me the dean of our school was shutting down the recreation administration program, which would mean losing my job. So, I started pulling in my network and working out the arguments in my head that I would present. Finally, I mentioned it to our department chair, who wondered why I was all up in arms and corrected me with the truth.

Despite my wariness, the man got me again. Some things are just easy to believe and believe in, whether true or not.

Sometimes I'll encounter someone who does not believe in Jesus. They'll share with me other belief systems they have investigated. My advice to them is to keep seeking answers. I say it to them this way, "If you seek truth, it will find you."

In this cell call to the Colossians, Paul warned of such conspiracy theories harming the believers in that area. Paul struggled because he wanted so desperately to see them himself. But since he couldn't, as he was still in prison, he chose to write to encourage his friends in the faith.

Paul speaks of the mysterious plan of God and the treasures of wisdom and knowledge. He tells his friends that wisdom and knowledge could be theirs because God does not hide those things from His children. The false teachers of that time, or conspiracy theorists as I would call them, were teaching about hidden godlike mysteries not shared with ordinary people.

A CELL CALL FROM PAUL

In our current culture, there are so many "truths" available to people. It wasn't all that different in biblical times. For example, check out this conversation at the trial Pilate held for Jesus.

> Pilate said, "So you are a king?"
>
> Jesus responded, "You say I am a king. Actually, I was born and came into the world to testify to the truth. All who love the truth recognize that what I say is true."
>
> "What is truth?" Pilate asked. (John 18:37–38a NLT)

As he reminded the Colossians, Paul would remind us to seek the truth when we hear stories that seem to hold a portion of the truth. If we ask the same question Pilate did, we come closer to discovering the truth of God, rather than a passing fad truth or conspiratorial truth.

Paul, very aware of conspiracies at that time, sent this cell call so that the people of Colossae would not allow deception by lies or conspiracy theories. Instead, Paul encouraged the people, much like I do, that it will find them if they seek the truth.

Want to take a trip with me? I have some free time since our dean canceled our program. I think I'll go to the Elvis Live concert and party with Bigfoot at the moon-landing site located at the edge of the earth.

What Is the Rule about Rules?

Colossians 2:6–23

My father had some of the weirdest eating habits, and it constantly evolved around peanut butter. He would tell my brothers and me that we could eat for a while on a loaf of bread and a jar of peanut butter when times get tough financially. He carried this love affair with peanut butter to the point that we often wondered if he might be insane. He would put peanut butter on pancakes and waffles before pouring syrup on top. He would mix peanut butter and syrup to spread on toast. However, the wildest version was his desire to put peanut butter and mayonnaise together with roast beef or hamburgers.

I thought he was delusional until I tried it. I choose to avoid the peanut butter on pancakes and waffles, but I regularly dine on the other concoctions he created with peanut butter. In a rare coincidence, someone on Facebook asked her friends about weird food combinations. I shared my dad's choice, and she saw it as being weird. Of course, her combination was peanut butter and pickles. Strange how peanut butter makes so many odd combinations. Whenever someone commented on his dining choices, Dad's reply was "Don't knock it if you ain't tried it."

I tried it, and I liked it. I understand Dad's use of the same reply. When you have a particular taste for a specific food, there is a judgment to follow. During my time at First Baptist Church in Springfield, Missouri, I was occasionally in charge of the youth mission trips. To save money, we didn't eat restaurant food except while we were on the road. I had a couple of people volunteer to prepare meals for us in the church kitchen where we were staying. I ordered my beef sandwich as my dad would have. After the initial shock, Nancy Good, one of our kitchen volunteers, said she saw how that could be good. A hamburger restaurant opened in Oxford a few years ago, and they featured a hamburger with peanut butter. I asked the server to add mayonnaise to it. She looked at me with judgmental eyes and asked, "Why would you want to do that?"

Another food judgment I have encountered in my life deals with barbecue. Having lived in three of the four areas with a reputation for good barbecue, Kansas City, Texas, and Memphis, I deem myself somewhat an expert in the tasting field. Visits to the Carolinas round out my barbecue expertise. Here's the rub on barbecue (pun intended): everyone has different and unique tastes. Some like sauce, while others prefer it dry. Some put coleslaw on the sandwich, while others don't. Some say pork is best, while others say it has to be beef. It's OK for one to prefer, but far too often, that preference becomes a judgment against someone who likes it differently.

There are food rules out there to follow. I've never seen them in print, but people tell me they exist. The use of peanut butter, beef or pork barbecue, coleslaw or not on the sandwich, ketchup or hot sauce on eggs, American cheese or ice cream on apple pie, and steak sauce on a steak are some of the eating rules that people have set and use to judge others.

I know specific rules are in writing that I must follow. God gave specific laws and commands that are not up to question. These are not the ones Paul is writing about in his letter to the church in Colossae. He's referring to the human-made rules that were circulating in the culture at that time. A quick review of history demonstrates the fear of exile for the nation of Judah made them dedicated to keeping God's law. To do so, they created a list of rules to define the rules God gave them. For example, they created rules to describe the commandment that we are to keep the Sabbath holy. The leaders made a list of what you could do on the Sabbath without breaking it. One of my favorites was that you could help your ox out of a ditch if it fell in, but if your wife fell in, you could not help her out.

That sounds silly, right? I thought so, and yet, when the exposure of secret sin took place in my life, I created a list of things I couldn't do to keep myself out of that sin choice again. Certain television shows, advertisements, movies, and travel routes were on the list to keep me away from sinful thoughts and actions. The list was OK to follow, but the list could do nothing about where my mind would travel, which is where temptations always begin. Instead of following the list legalistically, my accountability team had me memorize a section out of Paul's cell call to the Philippians about thoughts being true, honorable, right, pure, lovely, and admirable" (Philippians 4:8 NLT).

I find Paul's suggestions and guidelines much more helpful than my list, even to this day.

Unfortunately, Christians often do the same thing to determine how good of a Christian I am or another person might be. We created lists of daily Bible readings, outreach visits, attendance in church, leading in prayer, and how much one gives back to God in time, talent, and treasure (money). The Colossians were facing the same list-making emphases. The circumcisers of that time had afflicted this church as well. There was also a judgment about what Christians were eating and if they were participating in certain religious festivals. The people were less a Christian if they didn't participate in certain holidays or participated in others. The same judgment came with their made-up rules about what a follower of Jesus could and shouldn't eat. I remember dating a lady once who believed in opening Christmas gifts on Christmas Eve. I've been a Christmas-morning person all my life. Can you imagine if she questioned my level of commitment to Christ based on when I opened gifts? In a sense, that's what the rule reminders were doing.

These rule reminders were setting their standard of what it meant to be a Christ follower. Paul warned against the "well-crafted arguments" the rule reminders were offering. Paul tells us that we have died with Christ, and in that death, we are free from certain rules. Paul mentions three, those being "Don't handle! Don't taste! Don't touch!" (verse 21).

The danger I face when confronting the judgmental is that I become judgmental. Paul didn't recommend reverse judgment; instead, he advised the Colossians to ignore the pleas of those he called angel worshipers, pious, and proud, sinful-minded people. Paul pointed out that the list makers seem wise because their task list requires devotion, denial, and discipline. But, of course, Paul lets the Colossians know the list does not diminish one's evil desires. On the contrary, the list reminds us of where we have done wrong, leading to guilt rather than freedom in Christ. The time I spent with my list would affirm Paul is correct.

While the rule reminders want us to follow a list, or in that time, get circumcised, Paul points out the circumcision of the soul has already taken place in the death and resurrection of Jesus. The verse that points this out is 12a, "For you were buried with Christ when you were baptized. And with him you were raised to new life." I wish I had a dollar for every time I heard that scripture cited during a baptismal service. We have died to our sinful nature; therefore, we can toss some of the "don't touch, don't handle, and don't taste" rules.

Perhaps I should make a list of those. But, on second thought, let's not make a list. Oh, and please pull your wife out of the ditch. Otherwise, you might be in the barn with the ox.

Clothing Makes the Man!

Colossians 3:1-17

I met her on an online dating site. She lived twenty miles away and agreed to meet me at a restaurant in Oxford. In previous communications, she had confessed she had terrible luck on first dates. I tried to keep an open mind and not rush to judgment too soon on her. I arrived first and got the table. I texted where I was in the restaurant. A few minutes later, she came and was walking toward the table. I got up and gave her what I call a church hug. A church hug is done side to side, so there is no opportunity for trouble. She sat and said, "You seem shorter than you stated in your profile."

I offered that I was, indeed, five feet seven inches tall. The lady replied that she was five feet five inches and that it seemed like I wasn't two inches taller. I thought, *OK, make fun of a short man's height. Strike one.* Then she questioned my judgment on the choice of a restaurant. She had never dined there but was cynical as to why I picked it. *Weird. Strike two.* Without a moment's hesitation, she looked at my chest and then back up to my face and said, "Please tell me you didn't wear that to work today."

I admitted that I had, to which she said, "OK."

Well, I know when some women say, "OK," it does not mean OK. So, I asked if something was wrong with a light blue shirt and black slacks. Her comment was "If you have to ask, then you must not know."

Brilliant line of logic. Strike three.

A CELL CALL FROM PAUL

An old proverb states, "Clothing makes the man." The phrase has often been attributed to Mark Twain but is originally in the works of Erasmus and even earlier obscure works.[42] My light blue shirt / black slack combination told this lady something about me that caused her to question. Surprisingly, I didn't hang around long enough to find out what it was. Years later, I had a date question my clothing choices on the way to the restaurant. Another set of ladies told me I would never find a woman if I kept going out in public in blue jeans and casual T-shirts. If clothing makes the man, then apparently I'm not much of a man.

I have discovered people notice our clothing. Oh, and it's not just a few women I've dated. I wore a shirt on a Wednesday, did laundry that night, and put the same shirt on the next day. I didn't remember wearing it the day before, and the shirt was the first one I came to in the closet Thursday, so I wore it again. I had three people point out that I was wearing the same shirt as the day before. I couldn't convince any of them that I had laundered it.

During my college years, Tommy Burnett, one of my favorite professors, made it part of his lectures on professionalism to convince his class that we have to dress the part. We shouldn't show up to a meeting of the city's aldermen wearing our pickup basketball clothing. Professionals dress the part. On the other hand, when I saw a photo of a pastor at a softball game swinging at a pitch in a three-piece suit, I knew the other side of what Dr. Burnett was meaning about clothing making the man. In other words, what people see on you is what they'll believe about you.

One of my former students had her wedding in Hawaii. She wanted to fly me there so I could officiate the wedding. I asked her if she wanted me to wear my black suit, and she told me she'd prefer me to wear a Hawaiian shirt. I told her I didn't have one of those and doubted I could find one in Oxford. I could hear the sarcasm in her voice, which made me proud, as she said, "I think they might sell them over there."

---

[42] https://atkinsbookshelf.wordpress.com/2012/03/26/clothes-make-the-man/.

In my camp leadership class, we stress how to pack the proper clothing for the appropriate environment. Experts advise wool in cold weather. Cotton in cold weather leads to all kinds of trouble. I heard a riddle once about cotton in winter camping. The question is "What do you call a camper that wears cotton in a cold winter setting?" The correct response is "Dead." Even in camping, clothing makes the man. In my leadership class, I caution students to observe the clothing children wear. If they wear warm-weather clothing in cold weather or clothing with suggestive statements, it might signify parental neglect. In cases like those, clothing can definitely make the man.

In this cell call to the people of Colossae, Paul spoke metaphorically about the clothing we should wear as followers of Christ. Paul goes through a list of all kinds of behaviors that will not associate us with Jesus. Clothing such as sexual immorality, idolatry, worshiping material things, and greed. Paul suggests that we take off the clothing of anger, rage, maliciousness, lies, and dirty language. In other words, what people see on us leads them to believe whatever about us.

Instead, Paul says, put on the clothing of mercy, kindness, humility, gentleness, and patience. Paul says we should forgive those who offend us and offer grace with one another's faults. But, most of all, we should wear love. Clothing does make the man!

If we clothe ourselves in love, we present this world with a compelling argument to follow Jesus. Christ didn't hate those who disagreed with Him. Christ didn't hate those who didn't believe in Him. I believe the world would see a different picture of Christ if all of us followers wore the clothing Paul speaks of to the Colossian people. I wrote a blog years ago in an attempt to influence those who followed me in social media titled "Rights versus Responsibilities."[43] The point of the article was to remind followers of Jesus that His words did not say, "By your stances, they will know you belong to me." Nor was it, "By your political views, they will know you belong to me." Most of all, it was not, "By your boycotts, they will know you belong to me."

---

[43] https://dwaddell7.wordpress.com/2018/08/09/rights-versus-responsibilities/.

What Jesus said was "By this everyone will know that you are my disciples, if you love one another" (John 13:35 NIV). Clothes make the man.

In the next section of this cell call found in the third chapter, Paul reminds us how family relationships are better if we wear proper clothing. I'm one of those people who dress differently at home than I do in public. I look at old pictures and see myself in the same T-shirt and Kansas City Chiefs sweatpants. Even now, I have a favorite shirt and shorts to wear around the house. I write this as the world is going through the COVID-19 crisis. During the most severe time in the pandemic, our church services meet through YouTube and Facebook Live instead of gathering in the buildings that house our churches. Because I can log in to the service, I didn't worry about changing my comfortable around-the-house clothing. However, while listening to our discipleship pastor announce the return to live services, I thought he might need to remind everyone to change out of their around-the-house wear.

Comfortable clothing points out that those who live with me see me for who I am. The façade breaks down, the mask comes off, and I demonstrate the real me in real life. Paul reminds us that the clothing we wear at home, such as mercy, love, and compassion, reflects the love of Christ to those who are most important to us. Love helps us be better wives, husbands, parents, children, and servants. What people see on me is what leads them to believe about me.

Another phrase about clothing relates to maturity or dealing with challenging issues. That phrase is "Put on your big-boy or big-girl pants." If we are to convey God's love to our family, friends, and the world, we need to put on our love, mercy, and compassion pants and get on with life. Clothing does make the man!

Choose your spiritual clothing wisely, as someone will ask you, "Are you going to wear that?"

Who's the Boss?

Colossians 3:18–4:1

The Philippians and the Colossians had a few things in common. One must have been a reminder of how to serve the Lord when you are a husband, wife, father, mother, child, or slave. Since we covered that aspect in the Philippians verses, I want to concentrate on Paul's advice in this section of his cell call to proper protocol of a working relationship. Or, in other words, who's the boss? The key to employment situations is to remember Paul's words in verse 23, "Work willingly at whatever you do, as though you were working for the Lord rather than for people."

I've had more than a fair share of conflicts with the people I've worked for in various places. At times, I have felt they dealt with my coworkers or me unfairly. My attitude hasn't always been the best for those in authority over me. I find it easy to blame my employer or teacher for my unhappiness. I had and still have so much to learn.

You may want to hit those cheese and crackers, as I'm about to serve whine again. In the process of maturing and growing, I've had numerous snags in my life. One supervisor offered to reimburse me for a conference expense and reneged by arguing I was getting school credit for it. I argued that I had used my school credit for the previous year's conference, but I lost the argument and never saw the money.

Another supervisor changed my job description three times in one month before finally returning me to the original set of duties. Finally, I received a write-up from another supervisor for not looking busy enough during a church carnival. I argued that I wasn't doing anything because I had delegated all the work to various church members. He replied that I should have looked busy just the same.

My attitude to all of the above was to respond in sarcasm and bitterness. I allowed difficulty with my employer to ruin my experiences at those churches. I forgot who I worked for in reality.

One would think I'd get better as I get older, right? But, no, I'm still learning. For example, a few years ago, my department chair, in an attempt to benefit our graduate assistants with extra financial resources and teaching opportunities, decided to cut back the number of courses the faculty could teach in the summer sessions. Despite the personal loss, the faculty have all assisted the graduate assistants in planning their summer courses.

Selfishly, I liked the extra money, but in the process, I realized God is in more control of my finances than my employer is. God reminded me of what Paul told the Colossians in his cell call then and at various points in my occupational career. I may be listed as faculty at the University of Mississippi the same way churches or other employers listed me. These various entities were my employers, but they didn't control how much money I made or my level of satisfaction. Those attributes are under God's control. He is the one I work for in reality. See what Jesus had to say when Pilate claimed control of a situation:

> "Why don't you talk to me?" Pilate demanded. "Don't you realize that I have the power to release you or crucify you?"
>
> Then Jesus said, "You would have no power over me at all unless it were given to you from above. So, the one who handed me over to you has the greater sin." (John 19:10–11, NLT)

While serving at Germantown Baptist Church, the situation came where I needed to find an associate pastor of recreation to work with me and the team. This person would be primarily responsible for our sports and drama ministries. I realize it's an unusual combination, but I was looking for an unusual leader. Our pastor, Sam Shaw, encouraged us to look inward and consider possible church members for ministry leadership positions. He and Gerry Peak had already set the tone for this by hiring the children's and preschool ministers from the church membership.

I also put the word out in the usual manner through the Memphis newspaper and various online job search sites. As a result, I ended up with over two hundred résumés. In addition, I contacted other recreation ministers around the nation to obtain any networking possibilities. After all that, I decided that perhaps my pastor knew what he was doing and called John Longworth, a church member, about the available position. John tells the story in the book, *Putting the Church Back in the Game*.

> As I opened the door to my office, the phone began ringing. On the other end of the line was David, the recreation pastor at my church. The first words out of his mouth were:
>
> "John, you may think I'm insane ..."

I resisted the temptation to interrupt and affirm his suspicions and just listened.

> He continued: "Yes, you may think I'm insane, but have you ever considered working in recreation ministry?
>
> I couldn't resist a second chance.
>
> Yes David, I do think you're insane and, no, I've never considered working in recreation ministry."[44]

---

[44] Greg Linville. *Putting the Church Back in the Game: The Ecclesiology of Sports Outreach* (Press Canton, OH: Overwhelming Victory, 2019). *Author exchanged one word for more appropriate word in quote.

A CELL CALL FROM PAUL

Part of the story not included in that book was the final interview with John. John had already received the blessing of our personnel committee. Due to the unusual strain of church work, I always used the last interview with a candidate to include their spouse. Sandra and John met me at the Collierville, Tennessee, Applebee's for dinner and the concluding discussion before offering him the position.

John shared with me two goals he would aim for should we work together. First, he said he would do all he could to please and serve God. Second, he would do everything in his power to make me look good. At that point, Sandra chimed in by pointing out that John may have just given himself an impossible task with his second goal. John reminded her that this was an interview, and she said, "Yeah, but it's Dave."

They both grew in my admiration that day. John knew the words of Paul's cell call all too well. I will state here in writing that he did very well in attempting to accomplish both of his goals, although I made it difficult for the second part from time to time. John impressed the church enough that when I resigned, the church named him as the new recreation pastor, and he remains in that position to this day. Today, his goals remain: serve God, who he truly words for, the best he can, and make his senior pastor look good.

Who do you work for now? Oh, wow! We have the same boss!

If You Can't Say Anything Nice

Colossians 4:2-6

"Sticks and stones can break my bones, but words will never hurt me."

The above statement became a famous response to verbal bullying in English-speaking schools. The first citing of the phrase occurred in March 1862 in *The Christian Recorder*.[45] I learned it in elementary school and recited it in junior high when I faced some of my greatest bullying. By the time I entered high school, I had learned that the phrase was bogus. As a defense mechanism, I would find a person's weakness, be it physical, mental, or family, and strike the bully with words that would devastate them. Words can either hurt or heal. The intent of the communicator is what makes the difference.

I'm not proud of some of the things I said, but it did put an end to having fun poked at me for being short, skinny, and getting a late visit from puberty. By the time my sophomore year began, most of the bullying had gone away. I'm not sure if it was because others matured or they didn't want to challenge the word warrior. I learned from that experience that words matter.

I deal somewhat with a type of speaking disorder. My problem is my tongue works faster than my brain and any filters God placed in my system. You or someone you know may suffer from the same disorder. I've said things I meant to be funny, only to realize that it was instead hurtful once it was out of my mouth. For example, when

---

[45] https://www.phrases.org.uk/meanings/sticks-and-stones-may-break-my-bones.html.

my grandmother (Mom's mother) visited us, she talked to my dad about her estranged brother in California. For some reason, and to this day, I can't figure out why, I decided to repeat a phrase from a commercial and said, "Truisms aren't always true."

Grandma got emotional and started crying. I asked Dad what I had said, and his reply was "Something silly, as usual." More than fifty years later, those words still haunt me. I would never have wanted to hurt Grandma. Words matter.

Another phrase on this topic of words is "loose lips sink ships." This phrase was originally "loose lips might sink ships." During World War II, this phrase came into play to remind us that one does not want to give away any secrets by talking in places where others can hear. The slogan was first heard in 1942 and appeared in a Maryland paper, *The News*, in May 1942. Be careful what you say; after all, words matter.[46]

A related problem to the talking disorder of no filter and lousy timing is my ability to talk about other people behind their back. In some situations, it is to discuss what was said to the person, but it's simply to talk about them in many cases.

Yet another issue with my speaking troubles is the ability to use inappropriate words to express a feeling. This tendency occurs most when I am in a motor vehicle driving among other motor vehicles. For example, through some studies, the city of Oxford determined that traffic circles, or roundabouts, as they refer to them in the United Kingdom, are the best way to keep an intersection moving. The study they quote states traffic circles are faster than stoplights or four-way stops. I'd be more inclined to believe their statistics if someone also put on a nationwide educational tool to teach people how to drive in them.

If a car stops when it's supposed to go or goes when it's supposed to stop, it brings out the variety of language I rarely used when I was in church work. It was so rare that my sons told me they knew not to cross the line when one of those words popped out of my mouth.

---

[46] https://www.phrases.org.uk/meanings/loose-lips-sink-ships.html.

Before you judge me about using inappropriate language, please know that the substitute words some use instead of swear words carry the same attitude as those swear words. Therefore, you don't get a pass by using an acceptable word to express an inappropriate feeling.

I come by this ability honestly. My father had a favorite name for traffic offenders and others who frustrated him. He had a substitute word of his own and would call them a "slobknocker." Mom tells the story of my older brother just after he was getting a handle on the English language. Dad got frustrated with someone, and Allen said, "Dad, is he a slobknocker?"

According to my mother, Dad replied, "Why, yes. Yes he is, son."

Despite the slobknocker abilities shared in humanity, Dad would also tell us from time to time, "If you can't say something nice, don't say anything at all," which may be one of my favorite "watch what you say" phrases. During my childhood, it was in the Walt Disney cartoon *Bambi* that Thumper the rabbit's mother said the same thing to him. But, of course, as you can tell from the stories earlier in this section, I didn't pay much attention to my dad or Thumper's mother.

I feel sure some of you heard the same advice from your parents. I hope you listened more than I did. James, in his letter to the twelve tribes of scattered Jews, spoke of the untamed tongue. James mentions how we have tamed wild horses and can make them go where we want to go in the third chapter. We've made rudders whereby we can control the direction of a ship on choppy waters. James relates the tongue to the tiniest spark, which can destroy an entire forest. Even before Smokey the Bear got rolling, James warned about forest fires started by a loose tongue.

The power of our words, James continues, can praise God one moment, and in the next, the same tongue is cursing those who God created. I wonder if James ever had to drive a chariot in the Roman roundabouts? Words matter.

Paul gave similar advice about the power of words in his cell call. He spoke of the Colossians living in peace with their neighbors who didn't follow Christ. He advised them to speak with gracious and kind words. Paul knew others would be listening either at that point or hearing the story from the person later. Although Paul was in chains, he promised to continue talking about the great mystery of Christ's plan for others.

Words do matter. So, be nice.

Pass the Baton to the Team

COLOSSIANS 4:7–18

I never ran track. I possess an incredible amount of slowness. If I ever did something wrong enough that I would have to run away from the police, I figure I'd stand really still with my arms out to make it easier for them to handcuff me. A few years ago, my slowness was proven as I watched a videotape a church member made for my son in which the church's father-and-son softball team was playing. There were several men in the church with sons who were juniors or seniors in high school. Since I was the recreation minister, I put this group together for a church-sponsored men's slow-pitch softball league. If they handed out trophies for father-and-son bonding, we would have been world champions that year.

In the video, I come up to the plate for my at-bat. I hit the ball down the right-field line. Then the footage shows me running to first base. I reluctantly used the word *running* because it appeared to be in slow motion. I asked my son if I ran that slowly. His comment was "I think the tape makes it appear faster than reality."

I'm glad I could hand off my humor, wordplay, and sarcasm to my offspring.

While I may not be the fastest one ever, I am quite a fan of watching human beings who possess great speed. These past few years have brought this old Kansas City Chiefs fan some satisfaction. The group of wide receivers has the nickname "Legion of Zoom." Each receiver is considerably fast in running the forty-yard dash, which is one of the standards for judging the speed of football players. Track and field competitions have several events that feature speed. One of these speed events I enjoy, in particular, is the relay races. Speed is one component of the relay race, but of equal importance is the transfer of the baton from one runner to the next. Teams win relay races on the runners' speed and the efficiency of passing the baton from one runner to the next. The handoff or transfer to a teammate becomes one of the most crucial aspects of the race. It takes more work if the transfer doesn't happen quickly, smoothly, and without error.

Successful transfers are beautiful in any setting. On March 4, 1797, George Washington handed the leadership baton of the United States to the new president, John Adams. Adams served as the vice president for Washington's two terms. Then he won the presidential election of 1796. For the first time in political history, power had transferred without the death of the former leader or a violent overthrow. The story goes that, after the inauguration, John Adams was waiting for George Washington to exit the room first. The former president reminded Mr. Adams that he was now a regular citizen and that Mr. Adams, as president, should exit the room first.[47] Mr. Washington had control over his ego enough to let the new man shine as he should in his new position. Our nation celebrates that this transfer has occurred forty-five times since that day.

In Deuteronomy 34, we read about the death of Moses, and Joshua becomes the leader of the Israelites. Joshua and Caleb were the two spies who wanted to rely on God's power and take the land away from those who inhabited it at that time. Joshua worked under Moses until God chose him to take Moses's place and lead them into their new home. The transfer was smooth because Moses had "laid his hands on Joshua," signifying to the people that he would be their new leader.

In the first two chapters of 1 Kings, we read about King David handing the throne to Solomon. This transfer was a much more peaceful transfer than we see with some of the following kings of Israel and Judah, where murder caused the exchange of the baton, which was almost not the case. Another of David's sons, Adonijah,

---

[47] https://projectjohnadams.weebly.com/peaceful-transitions.html.

had declared himself king. Abiathar the priest and Joab, a key military leader in David's army, agreed to help Adonijah become king. David got wind of the deal and instantly named Solomon as the new king of Israel. When nearing his death, David took time to instruct and encourage Solomon to be a godly king.

In my career, someone else had previously held every position of leadership in that particular position. Each predecessor left the job peacefully to take on roles in other places. The transfer of leadership was smooth, with no overthrow or death involved. There were no ego difficulties with my predecessor desiring credit or attention. On the contrary, all of them were verbally supportive of me. When I departed my leadership position from the last two churches I served, both churches promoted my associate minister of recreation into the lead position for the ministry. The one in Springfield, Blake Hayworth, continues to serve in ministry at a church in nearby Ozark, Missouri. The leader in Germantown Baptist, John Longworth, assumed the role in 2003 and is still in that position as I write this book. Most churches have similar records of peaceful transfers in ministry leadership positions as God calls one person away from a particular place and calls another into that situation.

When my leadership class at the University of Mississippi discusses training the next generation, I always explain that every place of employment I ever left became better after I was gone. I attribute that to the level of expertise in my hiring. But, unfortunately, my students assume it's because there's no direction to go but up after me.

In a workshop at a conference for sports and recreation ministers, I heard a seminar leader state that a leader's job is not complete until they have trained the next generation or prepared the way for their successor. After requesting prayer, Paul concludes his cell call to the church at Colossae with some successors who worked with him and will soon take over the leadership efforts of the church. He goes through a list of people he is sending to the church to assist them. He also gives thanks to those who are ministering to him while he is in prison. I feel that many of these mentioned continued to lead the churches long after Paul was gone.

The first he mentions is a man named Tychicus. Paul knew this man to be impressive and praiseworthy. He was quite the encourager. Luke refers to him in the story told in Acts 20 as a travel companion of Paul. Tychicus and some others went ahead of Paul and met him in Troas. He was a messenger for Paul, as he delivered an up-to-date report on Paul's activities to the church at Ephesus and for Titus as well (Ephesians 6:21, Titus 3:12, and 2 Timothy 4:12). Paul had great confidence in Tychicus and utilized his commitment to Christ.[48] Paul also mentions he is traveling with Onesimus. We learn more about Onesimus in the letter to Philemon, but we note that Paul did not refer to him as a runaway slave in his letter to the Colossians. Instead, he called him a "faithful and beloved brother" (Colossians 4:9 NLT).

The next person that Paul mentions is Aristarchus. He was also a traveling companion. He served as a delegate from the church in Thessalonica to go to Jerusalem with an offering (Acts 20:4). Paul refers to him as a "fellow prisoner" in his letter to Philemon. He must have been an effective witness for Jesus, as tradition states he became a martyr in Rome under Nero.[49]

Epaphras is another man Paul mentions in this letter. Epaphras is called Paul's "fellow-servant" or his "fellow-prisoner." Under Paul's advice, Epaphras was essential in combating prevalent heresies in Colossae. Paul noted his perseverance as well as the power of prayer the man possessed.

Paul also does a kind of roll call mentioning Luke, Demas, Justus, and Mark (cousin of Barnabas) for their roles in ministering to him. The one I wish to concentrate on is Mark. He points out that he is the cousin of Barnabas, so the people will know exactly which Mark it is. I take note because this occurs after Paul and Barnabas's rift regarding a younger, more immature Mark in earlier journeys. Paul, set to take off on another missionary visit, invited Barnabas to join him. Barnabas wanted to take Mark, which set off a disagreement between the missionary pair. Paul ended up taking Silas, and Barnabas took

---

[48] https://www.gotquestions.org/Tychicus-in-the-Bible.html.
[49] https://www.biblegateway.com/resources/encyclopedia-of-the-bible/Aristarchus.

Mark (Acts 15:36-40). Mark's attendance with Paul is a sign of grace demonstrated by Paul in bringing him back into a relationship with him. Mark went on to do great things for the work of Christ. Some of you may have read his reports on the life of Christ in a Bible book named after him.

He also explicitly mentions Nympha, who many believe to be a woman who housed the church of Colossae. Women were crucial to the work of the early church. There were no church buildings as we worship in today. Instead, churches met in someone's home. Finally, Paul mentions Archippus. Paul issues a word of encouragement to Archippus to stick with the ministry. Tradition indicates Archippus was a church leader in Laodicea.[50]

In closing the letter, Paul requests his cell call to be sent to the church in Laodicea to be encouraged. I hope the Colossians didn't see this as a chain letter type of request. Thankfully, Paul didn't offer good luck or bad luck for forwarding the cell call. I trust the church at Laodicea received the news and continued their prayers for Paul.

What baton are you handing off or receiving? Who will step into your shoes? Prepare them well.

---

[50] https://www.gotquestions.org/Archippus-in-the-Bible.html.

PAUL'S LETTER TO
PHILEMON

This letter is unique because Paul sent it to one individual rather than a church body. Philemon was active in the church in Colossae. Since Paul had never been to Colossae, most scholars feel he met Philemon elsewhere, possibly Ephesus.[51]

Paul hits on the relationship he has with Philemon. More than likely, Philemon came to know Christ through Paul's influence. A slave of Philemon's named Onesimus had run away and found Paul in the Roman prison. There, Onesimus became a follower of Jesus as well.[52]

Paul uses love to influence Philemon more than wielding an apostolic hammer. He implores Philemon to do the right thing in forgiving this man who was once a slave and is now a brother.[53]

---

[51] Thompsons, p. 1544.
[52] https://www.theologyofwork.org/new-testament/colossians-philemon/introduction-to-colossians-and-philemon/background-on-colossae-and-the-colossians.
[53] https://www.1517.org/articles/the-gospel-according-to-pauls-letter-to-philemon.

The Lender Becomes the Prisoner
PHILEMON

I have never lived in a house long enough to pay it off entirely. I have, however, wholly paid off nine automobiles in my life. I understand the ultimate joy of paying back a loan. I tend to make the experience a celebration when I mark that last car payment to the bank. I am planning an even greater celebration for when my current house gets paid off. There have also been numerous times when my credit card balance grew more extensive than it should. When I got to the place where I could make a payment that left a zero credit card balance, it felt like a significant accomplishment. There is a feeling of financial freedom to get rid of the debt.

In my first book, *Characters of the Bible: Finding My Stories in Their Stories*, I share the story of another way I had debt removed from my life. I had borrowed money from my father for education expenses, a 1971 Gremlin, and an engagement ring.

> I approached my college graduation night. The world awaited me. I had a new wife and had been accepted into the seminary for my graduate work. I knew money would be tight, but that is life. I walked through the line and got the diploma case and shook the hands of the university president. Yet this huge debt clouded some of the dreams and excitement in my heart.

I approached my dad following the "Pomp and Circumstance" finish of the ceremony, and he told me, "Your graduation present is that your debt is forgiven. Consider it paid in full."[54]

In one move, my dad removed one of the burdens in life. He gave me a sense of freedom that was incredible. The freedom of having no debt is one that I have enjoyed several times in life. I have no doubt it gave my father great joy to be able to wipe the debt clear. Likewise, God has granted me the same opportunity to "loan" money to my sons with no expectation of reimbursement.

Jesus told a story about a man who owned a good portion of a debt to another. When the man went to beg for grace, the lender forgave the loan. Then, in a wild turn, the one who had received loan forgiveness demanded immediate payment from one who owed him a smaller amount (Matthew 18:23–34). When I recall this story, I realize the one forgiven of a massive debt was not yet free. He was still a slave to finances because he couldn't pass the forgiveness to others. This story is essential in understanding the prison Paul discusses in his cell call to Philemon.

I have experienced this same feeling as expressed by the story Jesus told. There have been times in my life when God blessed me financially to where I felt the freedom to loan money to those in need. One of those experiences was when I saw on social media that a friend was hurting financially. I sent a private message to inquire as to whether I could help. The response was an emotional and affirmative one. I sent the money and felt a sense of freedom and blessing that I could do so. Then I saw the post where my friend took a vacation one week later to the beach. My blessing disappeared, and a feeling of righteous indignation replaced it. How dare they talk of the inability to pay rent or buy groceries and then spend the money I gave them on a frivolous vacation? I realize now when this and other similar occurrences took place, I not only gave up some money, I

---

[54] David Waddell, *Characters of the Bible: Finding My Stories in Their Stories* (WestBow Publishing, 2015).

gave up my freedom and exchanged it for a prison of frustration, impatience, and displaced anger. I call the anger displaced because I put it on the debtor, but I was actually angry with myself. My concern for repayment did not allow me to enjoy the original blessing of having enough funds to be a lender. Despite the grace shown to me in forgiven debt, I could not get past the feeling I was used and demanding immediate payback.

A few years ago, the phrase "pay it forward" was popular in our culture. The expression promoted the idea of receiving someone's graciousness and offering graciousness to someone completely different, giving with no thought of return or payback. I have been both the recipient and donor in these situations. During the time between my departure from church work and my position as a college instructor, there were numerous times I gathered enough cash to enjoy a meal at a restaurant. It was such a joy to discover that a random stranger or hidden friend purchased my meal. The money I gathered for the meal could pay for gas, utilities, or go toward rent. Instead of worrying about the return of the money I loan, perhaps I should look at it as a paying forward moment. This attitude will free me from being enslaved to the very thing that freed me. I won't complain, however, if the person chooses to pay me back. Imagine me with a quirky smile on my face right now.

While in prison, Paul gave a personal cell call to Philemon that made it into the New Testament. Paul thanks Philemon for his dedication to the Gospel and the unique sense of joy and encouragement he received from his friend. Philemon had a deep love for those who followed Jesus and in some way greatly influenced Paul as well. Philemon probably hosted a church in his home. His name in Greek means "affectionate." He was more than likely affluent, in that he owned at least one slave.

Paul had an excellent reason for writing beyond the initial greeting and encouragement. While in prison, Paul received a visit from a man named Onesimus, a runaway slave Philemon owned. Paul decided to send Onesimus back home but wanted to clear the path against any retaliation against the slave. It was during his visit with Paul in prison that Onesimus found his faith in Christ. Therefore, Paul told Philemon he ran away as a slave but was returning as a brother. Paul also reminded Philemon that his standing with God was due to Paul's ministry as much as it was for Onesimus. Finally, Paul asked Philemon to pay forward what he had received from Paul in this part of his cell call. In other words, I led you to freedom in Christ; therefore, you can lead Onesimus to freedom in Colossae.

My belief is Paul wanted to free Philemon from a lender prison as much as he wanted to free Onesimus from a slavery prison. Paul saw both men as being equally free in Christ Jesus. This view of equality has taken humanity a long time to grasp; however, Paul set up the idea that we should give up owning another person if we follow Christ. Instead, we should look at others as our brothers and sisters, as we all belong to God as His children. Unfortunately, it took the followers of Christ several centuries to realize this truth.

I think Paul knew that if Philemon desired punishment for his slave running away, then he exhibited signs that he was more enslaved than Onesimus. Paul even offered to pay it forward in his offer to cover any expenses that occurred in the slave's absence. I gather Paul wouldn't have worried about being paid back like I have so many times. Paul, while in prison, knew how to be free. I can also reason that Paul didn't worry about how Philemon would spend that money in the way I watched my borrowers.

If you find yourself in a lender's prison today, I hope the words in Paul's cell call to Philemon will encourage you. They certainly guide me. Step out of that prison cell! Life is so much better in freedom.

Conclusion

One of the great joys I find in studying the Bible and writing is how connected an ancient book is to our current culture. The words Paul sent in his cell call apply to our culture's narrative so well.

I hope this book will help you experience the grace and love God has for you without jumping through any hoops or bureaucratic steps. Remember, it is not our stances, politics, or other aspects that determine our identity in Christ. So, let's not make an issue become the new circumcision.

Practice Mr. Roger's silent moment and add to it the moment where you contemplate the influence and impact you have in this world.

As Paul would sign off, "Peace be with you, dear brothers and sisters, and may God the Father and the Lord Jesus Christ give you love with faithfulness. May God's grace be eternally upon all who love our Lord Jesus Christ" (Ephesians 6:23–24 NLT).

For more of David Waddell's writing, please check out https://www.westbowpress.com/bookstore and search "David Waddell," http://davidwaddell.biz/books, or https://www.amazon.com/David-Waddell/e/B01AKULJCC.